(1) WHICH CHINESE ANIMAL SIGN HAS THE BEST CHANCE OF BECOMING FAMOUS?

(2) WHICH SIGNS MAKE THE MOST DANGEROUS MATCH—IN LOVE OR FRIENDSHIP?

(3) WHICH SIGN IS A BORN PERFECTIONIST?

Unlike most other guides, CHINESE ASTROLOGY is written by a Chinese expert using the true principles that have endured for thousands of years. With her deep knowledge of this ancient art of divination and prediction, Sabrina Liao gives you an accurate, eye-opening reading of your personal sign. In addition, she tells you:

* The history and legends of Chinese astrology.
* How the five elements—metal, wood, water, fire, earth—further determine your fate.
* And more!

OPEN THE DOORS INTO YOUR HIDDEN SELF WITH . . .

CHINESE ASTROLOGY

by Sabrina Liao

(1) Monkey (2) Tiger and Sheep (3) Dragon

CHINESE ASTROLOGY

ANCIENT
SECRETS FOR
MODERN LIFE

SABRINA LIAO

WARNER BOOKS

A Time Warner Company

WARNER BOOKS EDITION

Cover design by Rachel McLain
Cover illustration by Jill Karla Schwartz
Book design and text composition by L&G McRee

Warner Books, Inc.
1271 Avenue of the Americas
New York, NY 10020

Visit our Web site at
www.twbookmark.com

 A Time Warner Company

Printed in the United States of America

First Paperback Printing: January 2001

10 9 8 7 6 5 4 3 2 1

To my father, Kevin Liao
my mother, Shirley Ni
and
my sister, Eliza Liao

Thanks for letting me be your little girl,
so
    I can
        become
            who I want to
                be

Contents

THE ANIMAL SIGNS
Personality characteristics, the Animal, the Person,
the Male, the Female, at Work, Best Occupations,
Famous People, Compatibility and Conflict,
The Five Elements

CHINESE
ASTROLOGY

Introduction

It all started with a paper place mat from a Chinese restaurant on Bleecker Street. It was a humid summer night in New York City in 1995. My friends, Eva, Philip, Reggero, and I were sitting at the corner table, when Philip started to read the paper place mat in front of him.

"Hey, I am a Dragon in Chinese astrology!" Philip declared, excited by this discovery. Then he asked me, "So, what does it mean to be born as a Dragon?"

As a Chinese who grew up in Taiwan, I was fortunate to know the basics about Chinese astrology, and replied, "As the celestial animal and symbol of the Chinese emperors, the Dragon is believed to be a powerful heavenly creature that will bring honor and prosperity to the family. This is why, in old times, every Chinese parent prayed in hopes of having a Dragon child born into the family."

Philip was quite satisfied with my short description, and seemed extremely proud to be a Dragon man. The next thing I knew, everyone turned to me to learn more about his or her own sign in Chinese astrology. I must say that I was surprised to discover my friends' fascination with this subject. And, with their encouragement I began my research on Chinese astrology and put up a small web site on the Internet to share my culture with the world.

My site, Sabrina's World: When East Meets West, http://cat.nyu.edu/liaos/horoscope.html was officially launched in Fall 1995. Since then, the site has received extensive exposure from the media, including CNN, BBC, the *Asian Wall Street Journal*, and AOL and has been viewed by millions of people. Through the years, I have received thousands of e-mail requests for more detailed information. Now, by publishing this book, I am hoping to feed all the curious minds out there and bring them one step closer to Chinese culture.

THE HISTORY

So, what is Chinese astrology anyway? Chinese astrology is an ancient art, which uses the time of birth, including the year, month, day, and time, to reveal insights into a person's personality traits, lifestyle, health, career direction, and compatibility with others. Although the exact origin of the system is unknown, Chinese astrology has guided the Chinese for over five thousand years and has a profound influence on our lives.

The Chinese system of zodiac is actually based on a ten-year Sun-Moon cycle that conforms to the ancient Chinese agricultural calendar. The cycle is divided into the five elements: Water, Wood, Fire, Earth, and Metal as well as the twelve animals, which represent each year. The system is influenced by Yin (female) and Yang (male) cosmic force, which is said to be an interpretation of universal harmony and balance.

THE LEGEND

Every time I've told someone, "You were born in the year of the Snake" or "You are a Rat" (this should be said nicely with a smile if you consider that person a friend), I've actually seen their expression instantly transformed ranging from pure curiosity to pure disappointment. In their own imagination, they probably related the Snake with the evil slimy python hissing at the poor helpless chicks on the Discovery Channel; or perhaps they recalled that sneaky despicable rat terrorizing their comfortable house, which they'd tried to catch for months.

So, of course they are disappointed. After all, a rat or a snake does not sound nearly as fascinating as a mythical dragon. But in reality, the Rat and Snake are well respected in China. The Rat is smart, inventive and certainly knows how to stash food, while the Snake is described as a charming and charitable creature in many Chinese folk tales.

So, the next logical question is, how were the twelve animals chosen? And why is the Rat first among the dozen? At first glance, some choices seem a little odd, but if you look back to 2637 B.C. in China and think about the agricultural society existing then, you will understand why these animals were selected. The Chinese used familiar rural animals of the time that had distinguishing characteristics to represent years with similar tones.

Nevertheless, there are still various folk tales regarding how the animals were selected. Among all the variations, there is one fascinating legend that has been passed down for generations. I don't really remember how I learned this story, but as far as I know, this is probably the most popular folk tale about Chinese astrology.

Legend has it that once upon a time, the Heavenly God realized that there hadn't been a system to keep track of time, so he decided to develop a calendar system. One day, he summoned the Earth God to hold a race for the animals inhabiting the earth. So the Earth God gathered all the animals, and announced that the first twelve animals to cross the river would be the signs in the zodiac calendar. What a great honor to be in the zodiac calendar! All the animals chattered excitedly, and all wanted to join the race to win their spot in the calendar.

After the announcement, the Cat turned to his best friend the Rat to express his deep concern. "How can I cross the river when I am afraid of water?" At the same time, the old Ox grumbled to himself, and said, "How can I cross the river with my poor eyesight?"

The intelligent Rat looked at the Cat, then the Ox, and then a brilliant idea entered his mind, "I've got it! We can hop on the Ox's back to guide him, and he can carry us across the river without us getting wet!" All three of them agreed this was a great plan. So, early before dawn on race day, the Rat, the Cat, and the Ox were cruising slowly in the river, leaving all the competition behind. Just as they reached the middle of the river, the calculating Rat sneaked up behind the unsuspecting Cat and pushed him off the back of the Ox into the river.

Unaware of the commotion on his back, the hard-working Ox paddled straight ahead and finally reached the shore. Instantaneously, the aggressive Rat jumped off the back of the Ox and raced to cross the finish line first, while the serious, enduring Ox finished in second place.

At the same time, all the other animals were struggling to cross the river. The courageous Tiger raced to the finish line in third place; the Rabbit, the Dragon, along with the

Snake also reached the finish line. The Horse arrived with the artistic Sheep. The Monkey was given ninth, the Rooster tenth and the Dog came in eleventh.

Meanwhile, the Heavenly God counted the animals and suddenly realized they were one animal short. At this moment, the meticulous Pig arrived just before the race came to an end and was given the twelfth spot. A moment later, the poor Cat arrived soaking wet and found out he was too late to win any place in the race. Needless to say, from that day on, the Rat has been the Cat's sworn enemy.

In the end, the Heavenly God was quite pleased with the results and gladly gave each animal a year of its own, bestowing the nature and characteristics of each animal to those born in that year.

SO, HOW DO YOU USE CHINESE ASTROLOGY?

For centuries, Chinese astrology has been deeply rooted in Chinese culture. When you ask someone for their age, they will most likely tell you their zodiac sign instead of their exact age. It is believed that one's sign has significant influence over one's personality and future. Some might question if this means that all the millions of people born in the same year will share the same personality traits? Although this may seem almost impossible, I have actually recognized many shared personality traits among friends of the same sign. Nevertheless, Chinese astrology is more complicated than the twelve zodiac signs, it is determined not only by the year you were born, but also by the hour of birth, Yin/Yang and the five elements. In fact, Chinese astrology can be very detailed and specific if you want an accurate prediction. Even today, most Chinese people still rely on Chinese astrology as a reference for decisions about compatibilities, marriage, career, and personality.

To start your education in Chinese astrology, you must first find out your own zodiac sign. As your sign is determined by your birthday in the lunar calendar, you should first look up your year as well as the element for that particular year. The Chinese New Year denotes the start of the calendar, so those born in the months of January and February should pay more attention to the start and end dates for that particular zodiac year to ensure the accuracy of their own sign.

THE FIVE ELEMENTS

Chinese believe that the five basic elements, Wood, Fire, Earth, Metal, and Water form everything in the Universe. As a fundamental part of the Oriental philosophy, the five elements are divided into Conducive and Controlling interrelationships.

A Conducive interrelationship means that these five elements will produce one another and help nourish each other. We get Fire from Wood because fire is produced by burning wood. We get Earth from Fire because fire can burn everything into ashes (earth). We get Metal from Earth because all metal has to be extracted from the earth. We get Water from Metal because metal will change into liquid when heated. And, from Water we get Wood because water nourishes plants, thus producing wood.

A Controlling interrelationship means that these five elements can control or be destroyed by another element. Wood controls Earth because trees draw nourishment out of the earth. Earth controls Water because the earth can absorb water and also blocks the flow of water through man-made dykes or naturally occurring phenomena. Water controls Fire because the water is used to put out fires. Fire controls Metal because the heat of a fire can melt metal. And, Metal controls Wood because trees can be chopped down by the metal blade of an ax.

Under this philosophy, no element is considered the strongest or weakest. Each element is either controlled by another element or can produce another element. In fact, they are dependent on one another and therefore, are considered equal.

In Chinese astrology, during the complete sixty-year cycle, each of the animal signs is combined with the five main elements: Wood, Fire, Earth, Metal, and Water. The element of your zodiac sign will exercise its influence on your life.

THE FORCES OF YIN/YANG

Since ancient times, the Chinese have believed that two major forces, the Yin and the Yang, control the universe. These two forces are the foundation of Chinese philosophy, people, and even Chinese medicine. Generally speaking, the Yin signifies death whereas the Yang indicates life.

Yin	Yang
Death	Life
Night	Day
Moon	Sun
Feminine	Masculine
Passive	Active
Cold	Hot

A well-known symbol called "Tai Chi" (the ultimate matter) embodies the Yin and the Yang.

In the circle, the two forces equilibrate the energy and keep everything balanced. No force is stronger or weaker than the other, when one is at its highest, the other is at its lowest. Together the Yin and the Yang become a whole and thus keep the universe in harmony.

CALENDAR

In order to identify your own sign, you must:
1) Locate the year you were born. (i.e. 1900)
2) On that row, check when your birth year begins and ends to see if your birthday falls into that lunar year. (i.e. 31 Jan. 1900 – 18 Feb. 1901)
3) If you do fall into that lunar year, identify your zodiac sign as well as your element.(i.e. Sign=Rat, Element=Metal)
4) Voilà! Now you can go to your zodiac sign and read the description! And then look up your family and friends and check their personalities and compatabilities.

Year	Year Begins	Year Ends	Sign	Element
1900	31 Jan 1900	18 Feb 1901	Rat	Metal
1901	19 Feb 1901	7 Feb 1902	Ox	Metal
1902	8 Feb 1902	28 Jan 1903	Tiger	Water
1903	29 Jan 1903	15 Feb 1904	Rabbit	Water
1904	16 Feb 1904	3 Feb 1905	Dragon	Wood
1905	4 Feb 1905	24 Jan 1906	Snake	Wood
1906	25 Jan 1906	12 Feb 1907	Horse	Fire
1907	13 Feb 1907	1 Feb 1908	Sheep	Fire
1908	2 Feb 1908	21 Jan 1909	Monkey	Earth
1909	22 Jan 1909	9 Feb 1910	Rooster	Earth
1910	10 Feb 1910	29 Jan 1911	Dog	Metal
1911	30 Jan 1911	17 Feb 1912	Pig	Metal
1912	18 Feb 1912	5 Feb 1913	Rat	Water
1913	6 Feb 1913	25 Jan 1914	Ox	Water
1914	26 Jan 1914	13 Feb 1915	Tiger	Wood
1915	14 Feb 1915	2 Feb 1916	Rabbit	Wood
1916	3 Feb 1916	22 Jan 1917	Dragon	Fire

Year	Year Begins	Year Ends	Sign	Element
1917	23 Jan 1917	10 Feb 1918	Snake	Fire
1918	11 Feb 1918	31 Jan 1919	Horse	Earth
1919	1 Feb 1919	19 Feb 1920	Sheep	Earth
1920	20 Feb 1920	7 Feb 1921	Monkey	Metal
1921	8 Feb 1921	27 Jan 1922	Rooster	Metal
1922	28 Jan 1922	15 Feb 1923	Dog	Water
1923	16 Feb 1923	4 Feb 1924	Pig	Water
1924	5 Feb 1924	24 Jan 1925	Rat	Wood
1925	25 Jan 1925	12 Feb 1926	Ox	Wood
1926	13 Feb 1926	1 Feb 1927	Tiger	Fire
1927	2 Feb 1927	22 Jan 1928	Rabbit	Fire
1928	23 Jan 1928	9 Feb 1929	Dragon	Earth
1929	10 Feb 1929	29 Jan 1930	Snake	Earth
1930	30 Jan 1930	16 Feb 1931	Horse	Metal
1931	17 Feb 1931	5 Feb 1932	Sheep	Metal
1932	6 Feb 1932	25 Jan 1933	Monkey	Water
1933	26 Jan 1933	13 Feb 1934	Rooster	Water
1934	14 Feb 1934	3 Feb 1935	Dog	Wood
1935	4 Feb 1935	23 Jan 1936	Pig	Wood
1936	24 Jan 1936	10 Feb 1937	Rat	Fire
1937	11 Feb 1937	30 Jan 1938	Ox	Fire
1938	31 Jan 1938	18 Feb 1939	Tiger	Earth
1939	19 Feb 1939	7 Feb 1940	Rabbit	Earth
1940	8 Feb 1940	26 Jan 1941	Dragon	Metal
1941	27 Jan 1941	14 Feb 1942	Snake	Metal
1942	15 Feb 1942	4 Feb 1943	Horse	Water
1943	5 Feb 1943	24 Jan 1944	Sheep	Water
1944	25 Jan 1944	12 Feb 1945	Monkey	Wood
1945	13 Feb 1945	1 Feb 1946	Rooster	Wood
1946	2 Feb 1946	21 Jan 1947	Dog	Fire
1947	22 Jan 1947	9 Feb 1948	Pig	Fire
1948	10 Feb 1948	28 Jan 1949	Rat	Earth
1949	29 Jan 1949	16 Feb 1950	Ox	Earth

Year	Year Begins	Year Ends	Sign	Element
1950	17 Feb 1950	5 Feb 1951	Tiger	Metal
1951	6 Feb 1951	26 Jan 1952	Rabbit	Metal
1952	27 Jan 1952	13 Feb 1953	Dragon	Water
1953	14 Feb 1953	2 Feb 1954	Snake	Water
1954	3 Feb 1954	23 Jan 1955	Horse	Wood
1955	24 Jan 1955	11 Feb 1956	Sheep	Wood
1956	12 Feb 1956	30 Jan 1957	Monkey	Fire
1957	31 Jan 1957	17 Feb 1958	Rooster	Fire
1958	18 Feb 1958	7 Feb 1959	Dog	Earth
1959	8 Feb 1959	27 Jan 1960	Pig	Earth
1960	28 Jan 1960	14 Feb 1961	Rat	Metal
1961	15 Feb 1961	4 Feb 1962	Ox	Metal
1962	5 Feb 1962	24 Jan 1963	Tiger	Water
1963	25 Jan 1963	12 Feb 1964	Rabbit	Water
1964	13 Feb 1964	1 Feb 1965	Dragon	Wood
1965	2 Feb 1965	20 Jan 1966	Snake	Wood
1966	21 Jan 1966	8 Feb 1967	Horse	Fire
1967	9 Feb 1967	29 Jan 1968	Sheep	Fire
1968	30 Jan 1968	16 Feb 1969	Monkey	Earth
1969	17 Feb 1969	5 Feb 1970	Rooster	Earth
1970	6 Feb 1970	26 Jan 1971	Dog	Metal
1971	27 Jan 1971	14 Feb 1972	Pig	Metal
1972	15 Feb 1972	2 Feb 1973	Rat	Water
1973	3 Feb 1973	22 Jan 1974	Ox	Water
1974	23 Jan 1974	10 Feb 1975	Tiger	Wood
1975	11 Feb 1975	30 Jan 1976	Rabbit	Wood
1976	31 Jan 1976	17 Feb 1977	Dragon	Fire
1977	18 Feb 1977	6 Feb 1978	Snake	Fire
1978	7 Feb 1978	27 Jan 1979	Horse	Earth
1979	28 Jan 1979	15 Feb 1980	Sheep	Earth
1980	16 Feb 1980	4 Feb 1981	Monkey	Metal
1981	5 Feb 1981	24 Jan 1982	Rooster	Metal
1982	25 Jan 1982	12 Feb 1983	Dog	Water
1983	13 Feb 1983	1 Feb 1984	Pig	Water

Year	Year Begins	Year Ends	Sign	Element
1984	2 Feb 1984	19 Feb 1985	Rat	Wood
1985	20 Feb 1985	8 Feb 1986	Ox	Wood
1986	9 Feb 1986	28 Jan 1987	Tiger	Fire
1987	29 Jan 1987	16 Feb 1988	Rabbit	Fire
1988	17 Feb 1988	5 Feb 1989	Dragon	Earth
1989	6 Feb 1989	26 Jan 1990	Snake	Earth
1990	27 Jan 1990	14 Feb 1991	Horse	Metal
1991	15 Feb 1991	3 Feb 1992	Sheep	Metal
1992	4 Feb 1992	22 Jan 1993	Monkey	Water
1993	23 Jan 1993	9 Feb 1994	Rooster	Water
1994	10 Feb 1994	30 Jan 1995	Dog	Wood
1995	31 Jan 1995	18 Feb 1996	Pig	Wood
1996	19 Feb 1996	7 Feb 1997	Rat	Fire
1997	8 Feb 1997	27 Jan 1998	Ox	Fire
1998	28 Jan 1998	5 Feb 1999	Tiger	Earth
1999	6 Feb 1999	4 Feb 2000	Rabbit	Earth
2000	5 Feb 2000	23 Jan 2001	Dragon	Metal
2001	24 Jan 2001	11 Feb 2002	Snake	Metal
2002	12 Feb 2002	31 Jan 2003	Horse	Water
2003	1 Feb 2003	21 Jan 2004	Sheep	Water
2004	22 Jan 2004	8 Feb 2005	Monkey	Wood
2005	9 Feb 2005	28 Jan 2006	Rooster	Wood
2006	29 Jan 2006	17 Feb 2007	Dog	Fire
2007	18 Feb 2007	6 Feb 2008	Pig	Fire
2008	7 Feb 2008	25 Jan 2009	Rat	Earth
2009	26 Jan 2009	13 Feb 2010	Ox	Earth
2010	14 Feb 2010	2 Feb 2011	Tiger	Metal
2011	3 Feb 2011	22 Jan 2012	Rabbit	Metal
2012	23 Jan 2012	9 Feb 2013	Dragon	Water
2013	10 Feb 2013	30 Jan 2014	Snake	Water
2014	31 Jan 2014	18 Feb 2015	Horse	Wood
2015	10 Feb 2015	7 Feb 2016	Sheep	Wood
2016	8 Feb 2016	27 Jan 2017	Monkey	Fire
2017	28 Jan 2017	15 Feb 2018	Rooster	Fire

Year	Year Begins	Year Ends	Sign	Element
2018	16 Feb 2018	4 Feb 2019	Dog	Earth
2019	5 Feb 2019	24 Jan 2020	Pig	Earth
2020	25 Jan 2020	11 Feb 2021	Rat	Metal
2021	12 Feb 2021	31 Jan 2022	Ox	Metal
2022	1 Feb 2022	21 Jan 2023	Tiger	Water
2023	22 Jan 2023	9 Feb 2024	Rabbit	Water
2024	10 Feb 2024	28 Jan 2025	Dragon	Wood
2025	29 Jan 2025	16 Feb 2026	Snake	Wood
2026	17 Feb 2026	5 Feb 2027	Horse	Fire
2027	6 Feb 2027	25 Jan 2028	Sheep	Fire
2028	26 Jan 2028	12 Feb 2029	Monkey	Earth
2029	13 Feb 2029	1 Feb 2030	Rooster	Earth
2030	2 Feb 2030	22 Jan 2031	Dog	Metal
2031	23 Jan 2031	8 Feb 2032	Pig	Metal

The Restless Rat

Ranking order   First

YEARS   ELEMENTS

1900 Jan.31	–	1901 Feb.18	Metal
1912 Feb.18	–	1913 Feb.05	Water
1924 Feb.05	–	1925 Jan.24	Wood
1936 Jan.24	–	1937 Feb.10	Fire
1948 Feb.10	–	1949 Jan.28	Earth
1960 Jan.28	–	1961 Feb.14	Metal
1972 Feb.15	–	1973 Feb.02	Water
1984 Feb.02	–	1985 Feb.19	Wood
1996 Feb.19	–	1997 Feb.06	Fire
2008 Feb.07	–	2009 Jan.25	Earth
2020 Jan.25	–	2021 Feb.11	Metal

Force:	Yang
Natural element:	Water
Season and principal month:	Winter—December
Direction of its sign:	Direct North 30 degrees
Hours ruled by:	11 P.M.–1 A.M.
Best companions:	Dragon, Monkey
Worst companions:	Sheep, Horse, Rabbit, Rooster
Color:	Black, White, Blue

PERSONALITY CHARACTERISTICS

Positive	Negative
Affectionate	Argumentative
Calm	Calculating
Charming	Defensive
Compassionate	Greedy
Dynamic	Gossipy
Experimental	Narrow-minded
Familial	Overambitious
Honest	Picky
Idealistic	Possessive
Imaginative	Quick-tempered
Intelligent	Restless
Open-minded	Secretive
Passionate	Selfish
Patient	Self-obsessed
Practical	Suspicious
Protective	
Quick-witted	
Sensual	
Sentimental	
Talkative	

RAT—THE ANIMAL

Most people probably have a negative impression about the Rat, the number one house pest. However, in Chinese astrology, as the first sign of the twelve, the Rat is viewed as a mixture of many things. He can be as friendly as the lovable Stuart Little, as calculating and intelligent as Jerry in "Tom and Jerry," as devoted and loving to his loved ones as the rats in *An American Tail*, or as mischievous and mean as in the *Mouse Trap*.

As mentioned in the introduction, the legend is that the Heavenly God awarded the first twelve animals that crossed the river to be the signs in the zodiac calendar. And it's just common sense that with the Rat's petite size and small feet, there is no way this tiny creature can win the race on its own. But as the story explains, the Rat won the race with its wits and intelligence.

As the first sign among the twelve in the zodiac, the Rat is considered a major sign in Chinese astrology.

RAT PEOPLE

You are quite ambitious and were born under the sign of charm and aggressiveness. Born optimistic, you seem to have a solution for everything. Friendship comes to you easily with your sense of humor and energetic attitude toward life.

It is very unlikely to find a Rat sitting quietly doing nothing. Rather, you are always busy and rarely have the luxury of relaxation. And even when you have time to sit down and enjoy a short break, your mind will still be running nonstop, planning your next grand scheme. However, you have the tendency to get bored easily with your projects and when that happens, you will simply shrug your shoulders, pull up another brand-new business plan you have been working on for weeks and yell, "Next" to move on to the next project.

You are very expressive and talkative. You like to go

to parties where you can spend quite some time chitchatting with your friends. Lively, sociable, and easy to get along with, it is not a surprise that you meet new friends every day.

However, as friendly and easy to get along with as you are, you are a very private person. The long list of names in your phone book does not mean you take everyone into your circle of friends. Actually, Rat people usually have more acquaintances than real friends. But to those who are close to you, you are a devoted and faithful friend. You revere and cherish them, and they will be treated as your family. However, as talkative and gossipy as you can be sometimes, you never confide in anyone. You are self-contained and often keep problems and secrets to yourself. You are extremely private and discreet when it comes to your own personal life.

On the surface, you might appear discreet or reserved, but if anyone looks deeper, they will find out that you are never as quiet as you may look. Adaptive and flexible, the Rat will survive in any situation. No crisis or defeat will take you down easily, and no challenge is too much for you. You will be successful in whatever you choose to do. And because of this remarkable ability to cope with difficulties, you are especially good at problem solving. You make a good adviser to others but not necessarily to yourself.

As a talented opportunist, you are always looking for opportunities, you are famous for your ambition and hard work. Quick-witted and smart, you know how to make the most of your time efficiently and usually get more accomplished in twenty-four hours than the other people do in as many days.

Sometimes mean, narrow-minded, and unsophisticated in outlook, you are also honest. And, as long as you manage to master your perpetual discontent and your insistence on living for the present moment, you can always make a success of your life.

You are confident and usually have good instincts. These qualities, combined with your stubbornness, mean you prefer to live by your own rules rather by others'. It won't be an easy task to work with Rat people. Why? Simple—because you are also a hundred percent perfectionist.

You have a talent for organization; perhaps this is why you usually make a good businessman or politician. Actually, the Rat seems to be the Scrooge of the Chinese zodiac. You count your dimes carefully and are known for your thrift and greed. Although there is an old Chinese saying that "being thrifty is a virtue," nevertheless, Rat people can appear downright stingy. You do not like to waste or throw anything away. You will be the type of person who will save every extra ketchup packet you collect from Kentucky Fried Chicken and keep every empty bottle after you finish your Evian. However, as frugal as you seem to be, you can be quite generous to yourself or the ones you love. For instance, when you really want something, you can become quite a spender. And you are very careful when you lend money to people. A little piece of advice to those who plan to borrow money from a Rat—read the contract carefully, or you might be paying three dollars interest for every dollar borrowed.

On the negative side, you are practical but lack courage. Sometimes extravagant and greedy, you are also gullible and can be taken by those less meticulous than you. And because you are a born opportunist and are constantly in search of ways to improve your wealth and lifestyle, if you are not careful you can be led into a mousetrap. Remember, don't let your greed blind you to danger and problems ahead.

Being first in the Chinese zodiac, you seem to be obsessed with being number one. Sometimes, you believe that you are better than others are, so you love to compete and conquer and always try to be the pioneer and the first in action. Your energetic nature tends to cause you to overload with tons of different projects, and this overambitious side of you can cause you to lose your projects because you have spread yourself too thin.

High-strung, you are clever, curious, and ever alert to your environment. Although you have the innate ability to sense danger, your greed sometimes overcomes your sound judgment and causes you to fall into the same trap over and over again. On the negative side, you like to criticize, nag, and compare. You can turn into a secretive, self-indulgent, and selfish creature when blinded by greed. In fact, most Rat people will probably suffer one major financial blow before they learn their lesson. In general, you must avoid being overambitious and learn to conquer your greed and quit while you are still ahead.

Rat people are not romantic, but you are sensual and loving. And Rat people can be hard to see through at first glance, because you are very protective of yourself. But it's worth sticking it out with a Rat; ask anyone who has a Rat for a lover, parent, child, or friend. You are very loyal and devoted friend.

THE MALE RAT

The male Rat is aggressive and intelligent. He lives by his wits and seems to have an answer for everything. At the same time he is friendly and easy to get along with, having a wide circle of acquaintances.

He is very determined, and once he sets his mind to something, it is very difficult to persuade him otherwise. He has business acumen and can turn any idea into a business plan. Perhaps this is his talent or his curse, but he is always on the run, looking for new ideas or working on new projects. Never sitting quietly or waiting aimlessly, the male Rat is a man with a mission.

However, he is also known for being overambitious. His passion for a project comes and goes before other people even have a chance to understand it, and he is always alert for the best opportunities. Constantly trying to do too much too soon, this busy male Rat tends to scatter his energy everywhere before he has any chance to finish one project.

The male Rat is a man with opinions, strongly believes in himself, and does not allow for other opinions when he is in charge. He'll ignore every warning sign he gets. In short, those people who are calculating can fool him because he often takes the bait when he thinks it will be profitable for him. This is probably why many Rat men experience at least one major downfall in their lives—greed and ambition can blind them to reality. Greedy as he sometimes appears, he is nevertheless honest. He earns his profit through his hard work and his intelligence, and never through tricks or cheating.

The Rat man is famous for his charm and wit and he likes to be the pioneer in everything. Sociable and fun, he possesses a good sense of humor and has an active imagination. He is very good with numbers, and this probably is due to his amazing intelligence and acumen in business. He is the type of student who is always the first to shout out the answer in class. When out drinking and dining with friends, the Rat will take the bill and quickly do the math, add the tax, the tips, and find out how much each person needs to pay in just a few seconds. And he actually really enjoys doing this and takes pride in his important role.

This fascination with numbers and talent of quickly calculating the odds in any situation indicates that this Rat man is a born gambler. Although he can be extremely thrifty to the point of being called a Scrooge, he can become almost extravagant under three circumstances. First, if he sees some luxury items he really wants. Second, when he buys gifts for his family and friends. Third, when he is in a casino. Since he is so confident about his talents for numbers, he believes he can beat the odds. So some advice for those close to a Rat man—keep him away from the casino.

He is very talented and intelligent. He is expressive, so all of his friends know about his talents. And, he loves to write down his thoughts and ideas. Several famous writers such as William Shakespeare and Leo Tolstoy were born in the year of the Rat.

In relationships, the Rat man is not really romantic. Don't expect him to shower his lover with flowers and sweet talk. After all, his practical mind will calculate the cost of the flowers and the number of days these flowers will last. Nevertheless, the honest Rat man can be trusted because he will always make his family his priority and will be extremely protective toward his loved ones.

THE FEMALE RAT

Just like the male Rat, the female Rat is witty and resourceful. A highly intelligent and creative person, the Rat lady can be a successful woman if she chooses to be.

With her excellent people skills, and fun-loving and compassionate personality, she is quite popular. She is fashionable but always elegant with her own style. Her environment is always clean and neat. A Rat woman's office will have her files neatly placed on the desktop, her calendar organized, and her table free of dust. It goes without saying that this Rat lady often manages her house the same way she does at work, which is probably why the Rat woman is considered to be an excellent candidate for a wife.

However, this does not mean the Rat woman is only quiet housewife material. In fact, she can be very business-oriented. She is keen and sharp and will automatically grab an opportunity when she sees one. Direct and honest, she is not afraid to speak her mind; but with her social skills, she knows how to say the right words so she will not offend anyone.

Surprisingly, the female Rat can be a true model of frugality. She certainly knows the virtue of recycling clothes, toys, furniture, and even soap. Again, like Rat men, she can be quite generous to her loved ones. So the children of a Rat woman will have no problem getting expensive toys for Christmas; Rat moms know how to take care of their children and are not stingy about the needs of their family.

Talkative and gossipy, the Rat woman is an inveterate gossip. Never trust your secret with her because she can't keep it long. However, she is very good at keeping her own secrets from others, and it is difficult to see into a Rat woman's mind. She is the kind of person who likes to keep her thoughts and feelings to herself; nevertheless, as a direct person, an angry Rat woman can be spotted even miles away.

The Rat woman is an avid reader, she is a lady who loves to read and can be found wandering around in Barnes and Noble bookstores or surfing Amazon.com. Moreover, she is a talented writer herself. At a young age she will learn of the importance of written words and probably be the editor for the high-school newsletter.

In love and relationships, she is tender and sensual. Also the practical Rat keeps her home tidy and organized. She will be a superb, loving mom who spoils her kids with toys, and also a dedicated wife who will follow her husband's career.

RAT AT WORK

Aggressive and ambitious, Rat people are extremely hardworking and do not know how to slow down. Born flexible and adaptive, Rat people can survive in difficult environments.

Always resourceful, Rat people make excellent advisers. They thrive in difficult situations and enjoy solving puzzles. In fact, Rats can usually come up with good solutions in a crisis. They can always count on their minds and wits instead of their physical strengths.

They have busy minds and are always on the run. Self-contained and self-preserved, Rat people can be neurotic about things at work but will behave calmly during a crisis. Rat people feel right at home when working in bureaucratic jobs; they like to stick to routines and disciplines.

As a boss, the Rat is very demanding. It is never easy to work for a Rat boss because they are often perfectionists and can be extremely picky. They are not as generous with compliments as they are with criticisms. However, with their born wits and talents, count on the Rat boss to lead a company out of a crisis.

As a partner, the Rat is extremely ambitious and not as communicative as they appear. Secretive and opinionated, their words are not easy to swallow sometimes because they are also very direct. Nevertheless, you can always count on the Rat partner to manage the finances because no one is more suitable to control the budget than a born Scrooge like the Rat.

As a colleague, the Rat is energetic. Working with a Rat can be a blessing or a curse. After all, anyone can always learn a thing or two when working with this efficient and productive person; however, at the same time, coworkers will be under a lot of pressure because of the Rat's excellent performance.

In general, with their imaginative wit and ambition, the Rat will do well as a financial adviser, writer, or musician. Claude Monet and Wolfgang Amadeus Mozart are just two famous Rat people.

BEST RAT OCCUPATIONS

Accountant	Lawyer
Antique dealer	Musician
Auctioneer	Painter
Broker	Pathologist
Confidential situations	Publisher
Connoisseur	Songwriter
Critic	Underground work
Detective	Writer
Financial adviser	

FAMOUS RATS

Antonio Banderas	Marlon Brando
Cameron Diaz	Plato
Claude Monet	Prince Charles
Franz Joseph Haydn	Sean Penn
Gene Kelly	Tchaikovsky
George Washington	William Shakespeare
Gwyneth Paltrow	Wolfgang Amadeus
Hugh Grant	Mozart
Jimmy Carter	

COMPATIBILITY

The Chinese believe each animal sign is most compatible with signs that are four years apart, and least compatible with the sign that is six years apart. Based on this concept, a circle can be drawn with all signs, locating the Triangle of Affinity and the Circle of Conflict.

TRIANGLE OF AFFINITY
Rat, Dragon, Monkey
These three are the best combinations in Chinese astrology

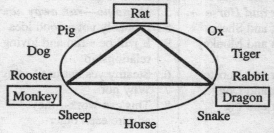

CIRCLE OF CONFLICT
Rat's conflict sign is Horse

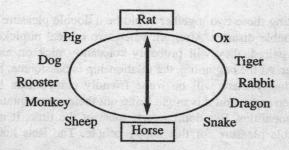

Signs	Rating 1–10	Relationship
Rat and Rat	8	A very good match
Rat and Ox	8	Lucky you two found each other
Rat and Tiger	7	In order to succeed both must endure
Rat and Rabbit	6	Nothing too exciting but it might still work
Rat and Dragon	9	One of the best-arranged unions
Rat and Snake	6	Better be friends than lovers
Rat and Horse	*3*	*No no no—run away now*
Rat and Sheep	5	Probably not a good idea
Rat and Monkey	9	It will be a fun and loving relationship
Rat and Rooster	6	Steamy yes but not lasting
Rat and Dog	7	Why not
Rat and Pig	8	This can work—they admire each other

Rat with Rat   *8*
A very good match

Putting these two together could be a double pleasure or a double disaster. After all, when two critical nitpickers are paired, they will probably constantly pick on each other. At the beginning, the relationship is passionate, but gradually there will be some friendly competition between them, and this might bring out their argumentative personalities. But don't worry, most of the time, it is a double pleasure for this happy couple. The Rats know how to put their intelligent heads together and make things happen. They see their partner as their best friend and dear lover, and because of their fear of loneliness, they will try to work out any obstacle to make the relationship work. Overall, the female is more critical and the male is more combative, so these two can make a great team.

Rat with Ox 8
Lucky you two found each other

Although these two share little in common, this will be an excellent, loving relationship. The Rat and the Ox share mutual love and understanding. The Rat will admire the Ox as a devoted partner, and the Ox will be attracted to this outspoken and intelligent Rat. They will be very sympathetic and compassionate toward each other, and they will enrich each other. Being the aggressive one of the pair, the Rat doesn't seem to mind the slow pace of the serious and diligent Ox. In fact, they can be great not only as lovers but also as partners. Lucky you to find each other.

Rat with Tiger 7
In order to succeed both must endure

When they first see each other, it will be love at first sight. The Tiger is attracted to the Rat's charm and liveliness while the Rat finds the Tiger alluring and lovable. But after the first spark of love fades, their relationship will have constant minor skirmishes. Both possess quick tempers and stubborn personalities, and both are too proud to compromise. Nevertheless, this relationship can still succeed, if they both make efforts to endure by communicating and learning to agree on their differences. In general, there is still hope for a long, loving marriage for these two.

Rat with Rabbit   6
Nothing too exciting but it might still work

Although there is no major conflict or special attraction between the Rat and the Rabbit, somehow, because of their differences, their relationship may not work too well. The Rabbit can be oversensitive while the Rat is overcontrolling. Both have high expectations of each other and this may cause more problems. This match may not seem to bring out the best in both personalities, but once joined, it will be difficult to separate this pair. Basically, it will be an amicable relationship and, in fact, sometimes these two make better business partners than lovers.

Rat with Dragon   9
One of the best-arranged unions

The Rat and the Dragon relationship is probably one of the best of all combinations. The Chinese believe this is the best match for both marriage and partnerships. The Rat will welcome the Dragon's dominance, and the Dragon will admire the Rat's intelligence. Both powerful and aggressive, they can work hand in hand to make things happen. Both self-confident and talented, they will not be threatened by the other. Their mutual admiration and support brings out the best in them. Whatever they do, as long as they do it together, these two will achieve success, happiness, and prosperity. This is an absolutely marvelous combination.

Rat with Snake   6
Better be friends than lovers

The Rat and the Snake can forge an interesting friendship together, but when it comes to a romantic relationship, these two have too much conflict and disagreement. Although both are intelligent and ambitious, these two approach life in very different ways. The Snake is a thinker who plans and schemes in detail while the Rat is actually an aggressive doer. They can be attracted to each other at the beginning, but as the infatuation fades, the Snake will pull away from the Rat and keep secrets to him or herself.

Rat with Horse   3
No no no—run away now

Being six years apart from the Rat, the Horse happens to be the conflicted opposite of the Rat. It goes without saying that these two are not only incompatible, but they'd better stay away from each other. The self-centered Horse can't understand the kind, sentimental Rat. Although they think opposites attract, the fact is that they see things from totally different perspectives. Eventually, the Rat will be craving more security, but the impatient and moody Horse just can't settle. Till the end, the Rat is most likely to be mistreated and suffer from the relationship.

Rat with Sheep   5
Probably not a good idea

The Rat and the Sheep can get along just fine, but the peaceful Sheep might find the restless Rat annoying at times. At the same time, the aggressive Rat will find the laid-back Sheep lazy. At first glance, their relationship appears calm, but underneath the surface, there is a cold war going on. Both the Rat and the Sheep are uncomfortable with confrontation and do not know how to resolve their problems. Nevertheless, their physical attraction is strong, and if they learn how to open up more and talk about their differences, there might be a slight chance for this relationship.

Rat with Monkey   9
It will be a fun and loving relationship

These two are highly compatible. Both are sociable party animals; they are bound to have fun and laughter together. This duo has much in common, and mutual interests and talents draw them to each other. They admire each other for their intelligence and creativity and share the same values and attitudes. They are likely to be dining out a lot because they have many friends to hang out with. On the whole, this relationship can be emotional at times, but there will be no dull moments when these two are together. The Rat should learn to accept the Monkey's dominance, and this would be lasting, intriguing, and one of the best relationships.

Rat with Rooster   6
Steamy yes but not lasting

When these two first meet, they see fireworks and sparks, but as the steam slowly fades, they will see each other more clearly, and disagreements will start to arise. In this combination, the Rat and Rooster will find themselves in constant debate over leadership. The Rooster can be extremely critical of the Rat, and the sociable Rat will get even with the Rooster by making the Rooster jealous. Eventually, it takes a lot of effort to keep the relationship alive.

Rat with Dog   7
Why not

The Rat and the Dog respect each other and can be an amicable couple. After all, they are both responsible and diligent and take their relationship seriously. Sometimes, the Rat might find it difficult to understand the sentimental Dog for the idealistic Dog can be too generous and tend to give money away. The practical Rat will be anxious over the money and try to save as much as possible. In the end, these two will know how to resolve their problems and learn from each other.

Rat with Pig   8
This can work—they admire each other

This is a positive relationship. The Rat and the Pig are both sociable and affectionate; they adore and respect each other. They work well as a team and are usually well connected and influential. The couple share the same passion for good food and vacation, and enjoy life as much as they can. The Pig is generous and sometimes has a great appetite for shopping. The Rat, however, is practical and thrifty. So in order to balance the relationship and their bank account, the Rat must take control of the purse and let the Pig charm the rest of the world.

THE FIVE ELEMENTS:
The Rat—the natural element is Water

THE METAL RAT: 1900, 1960, 2020

The Metal Rat possesses both softness from its natural Water element and inflexibility from the Metal element. They are likely to be idealistic and emotional. Metal Rats often appear charming and cheerful, but in reality they are capable of hiding their anger and jealousy.

The Metal Rat enjoys money and doesn't mind spending it on quality goods. This type of Rat likes to impress people with his or her classic taste and well-decorated home. The Metal Rat is generally ambitious and knows how to advance. One downfall is that they tend to be too rigid to creative ideas and are somewhat inflexible. They need to learn to be more open to compromise.

THE WATER RAT: 1852, 1912, 1972

The Water-Water combination endows the Water Rat with diplomacy and calmness. This type of Rat cares about the thinking process and mental awareness. They are usually very acute and observant, always knowing people's likes and dislikes. The Water Rats' understanding and accommodating nature helps them become great fashion designers that set the future trends.

The Water Rat is curious by nature and is always seeking knowledge and even higher education. Atypically, they are very sensitive to what others think of them, and sometimes agonize over nothing because of this. They should learn to be more forthcoming and learn to lead sometimes.

THE WOOD RAT: 1864, 1924, 1984

The Wood element brings creativity to the Rat. Wood Rats are mostly artistic and articulate. Driven by their passion to explore, they enjoy researching ideas and finding a good use for anything they come across. The capable Wood Rats know what they want and how they can achieve their goals. No wonder the Wood Rat is also very egotistical. Nevertheless, this type of Rat also learns to compromise and make themselves agreeable because they seek approval from others.

On the negative side, Wood Rats should recognize their limitations so they don't burn the candle at both ends.

THE FIRE RAT: 1876, 1936, 1996

The Fire element brings passion and enthusiasm into the Fire Rat. Often energetic and idealistic, the Fire Rat loves to get involved in all kinds of activities and projects. Open and aggressive by nature, Fire Rats often possess the luck and capacity for success.

Talkative at times, Fire Rats need to watch what they say. They can sometimes be too blunt and require some sense of diplomacy to win the support they need. On the negative side, this type of Rat can be too optimistic, and enthusiastic, which can sometimes lead to failure.

THE EARTH RAT: 1888, 1948, 2008

The combination of Water and Earth elements brings balance into the Earth Rat. Usually maturing early, this type of Rat seeks order, discipline and security. And because of this, they tend to work in one place or job for a

long time and refuse to change. They are very practical
and diligent, and care a lot about their reputation. Earth
Rats are family-oriented and can be very protective
toward the ones they love.

On the negative side, their inflexibility can slow down
their achievement and ambition, and sometimes, they can
be overpractical and stingy with money.

The Diligent Ox

Ranking order	Second

YEARS

ELEMENTS

1901 Feb.19	–	1902 Feb.07	Metal
1913 Feb.06	–	1914 Jan.25	Water
1925 Jan.25	–	1926 Feb.12	Wood
1937 Feb.11	–	1938 Jan.30	Fire
1949 Jan.29	–	1950 Feb.16	Earth
1961 Feb.15	–	1962 Feb.04	Metal
1973 Feb.03	–	1974 Jan.22	Water
1985 Feb.20	–	1986 Feb.08	Wood
1997 Feb.07	–	1998 Jan.27	Fire
2009 Jan.26	–	2010 Feb.13	Earth
2021 Feb.12	–	2022 Jan.31	Metal

Force:	Yin
Natural element:	Water
Season and principal month:	Winter—January
Direction of its sign:	Northeast 60–North 30 degrees
Hours ruled by:	1A.M.—3A.M.
Best companions:	Rat, Snake, Rooster
Worst companions:	Dragon, Horse, Sheep, Dog
Color:	Yellow, Blue

PERSONALITY CHARACTERISTICS

Positive	Negative
Authoritative	Biased
Capable	Chauvinistic
Careful	Cold
Clear-thinking	Complacent
Confident	Conservative
Conscientious	Dogmatic
Consistent	Dull
Creative	Easily agitated
Determined	Eccentric
Diligent	Gloomy
Eloquent	Hot-tempered
Gentle	Intolerant
Hardworking	Materialistic
Organized	Proud
Patient	Stubborn
Persistent	
Practical	
Reliable	
Serious	
Skillful	

OX—THE ANIMAL

For centuries, the Ox played an important role in the agricultural society of China. Born to serve, provide, and then be sacrificed, the Ox is one of the most precious assets in the farming community. In fact, in many villages where

Oxen work diligently in the field, farmers refuse to eat beef to show their gratitude to this hardworking animal that dedicates its entire life to the survival of the villagers. Even today, many Chinese still keep with tradition and do not eat any beef.

Aside from being a diligent worker in the field, the Ox actually became a matchmaker in one of the most romantic stories in Chinese mythology. The story begins with, once upon a time, there was a cowherd who was lied to by his greedy brother and then believed that the only property he had inherited was an old Ox that could no longer work. Suddenly one day this old Ox spoke to the cowherd, claiming to be a heavenly general; he then took the young man to a secret place, where he met and fell in love with a beautiful weaving fairy from Heaven. Their secret love affair eventually infuriated the Heavenly God so much that he summoned the fairy back to Heaven and ordered the lovers to be separated, with the Milky Way between them.

Heartbroken, the couple came to see each other day after day, but could only look across a great distance. Finally, their love moved the Heavenly God, who finally granted that they could meet one day each year. At last, the cowherd and the weaving fairy could meet once a year on the seventh day of the seventh moon over a bridge across the Milky Way formed by sympathetic magpies. Because of this romantic folk tale, the Chinese celebrate their Valentine's Day on the seventh day of the seventh moon each year.

Some say the actual birth time of year and day for an Ox will determine the lifestyle he or she will have. Usually, it is believed that the Ox born during the day will be more aggressive and active compared with the Ox born in the quiet night. Likewise, the winter Ox will have a more relaxed and easier life than the Ox born during agricultural months and sentenced to a life of hard labor.

OX PEOPLE

Born under the sign of loyalty and evenness, you are sincere, reliable, and fair. Just like the Ox who works hard and persistently in a field, you can stick to a task longer than any other sign, and can go at it harder than anybody. You are a conscientious worker and are quite dependable, calm, and methodical.

Highly accountable, you can be trusted with important responsibilities, and the truth is that you take these duties very seriously. And because of your steady and trustworthy character, you will slowly climb the ladder up to an eventual position of authority. Unlike the Dragon or the Monkey, who achieve their success through their talents and wits, you simply carry out your tasks quietly with persistence and diligence and earn your success by sheer tenacity and dedication.

You are quite famous for your courage, and you do not back down when facing obstacles or challenges. If you truly believe in something or someone, you are ready to fight for what is right despite the consequences. As a noble, conscientious, and determined soul, you view it as your duty to right the wrong and speak up when you see unfairness.

You are generally calm and placid, yet although appearing to be tranquil, in fact, you are also capable of fearsome rages and become explosive and impulsive when angry. It is not a pretty picture and can be quite terrifying; therefore, it is wise never to cross an Ox. Fortunately, you do not lose your temper easily, but in the rare moment when you do, your anger is mostly directed to those who are dear to you. For those people who happen to be around the angry Ox during a rampage of temper, the only advice is to "run quick, and look for cover." It is wise for everyone to keep as far away from the Ox as possible until they've cooled off. After all, a hotheaded Ox is like an angry Spanish bull that will charge at anything in its path as if the red flag is waving right in front of it.

Another side of you is that you are a born leader; you are dependable and believe strongly in yourself. With your innate ability and determination, you are able to achieve great things. Nevertheless, you are also quite stubborn and tend to classify almost everything into two basic categories—bad and good. In fact, you have solid opinions on everything, including people; you depend mostly on your first impression of an individual and will form an instant like or dislike. Most of the time, you will dislike someone for no apparent reason and refuse to give anyone a second chance.

You can be inflexible and dogmatic because you truly believe in your decisions and never have regrets. You take your words seriously and do not make promises easily. But once a promise is made, you will carry it out, no matter what. Unlike the impulsive Horse, who often follows only his or her heart, you follow your head. Although you can seem inflexible, you are filled with common sense and are willing to listen to advice from others. When it comes to important issues, you always weigh all the pros and cons before you make any final decision.

Ox people are not social or party animals; you tend to

be quiet when at a party. In general, you are not that social by nature and tend to become introverted in a crowd. You don't usually ask to be in the limelight; nevertheless, you do have a tendency to boss people around.

In many friends' eyes, you are a traditionalist and can be extremely rigid at times. Sometimes, it is not easy to be your friend because you hold up your high standards as a model, and severely judge those who don't desire to maintain these same standards. However, normally bright and patient, you are a good friend who enjoys helping others. Although you are easygoing and friendly and you trust your friends and colleagues, getting close to an Ox is a surprisingly difficult thing. Affectionate only to those who are close to you, you often appear cool and distant to anyone outside your circle of friends. You choose your close friends carefully; actually, most often it takes a long time for you to open up and establish a friendship.

Often you surprise your friends with your vivid memory and keen observation of details. If asked to remember who was at a party eight months ago, most likely you will name them one by one, adding a general description of what they wore and the gifts they brought.

Your home is very important. It is usually neat and organized, comfortable but not luxurious. Comfort is your top priority, and owing to your love of nature, you prefer living in a rural area rather than in a big city. If you are unable to live in the country, then it is essential for you to have a garden somehow. And probably it will be very well maintained because you like to do gardening work and enjoy working with the earth and growing plants and fruits.

Ox people are usually very close to their families. Even though you aren't easily moved by emotions, you are willing to sacrifice anything for the welfare of your family. At your home, your word is the law, you like to project an authoritative image and do not like to be challenged. However, you often find that those whom you are close to fail to understand you.

In romantic relationships, you are a very responsible and loyal partner. You are too honorable to permit any casual love affairs. Although you are not the romantic type, your feelings are deep and passionate. If you suffer a broken heart, you tend to retreat and be distant. You are famous for your tendency to nurture your grief far too long.

You are strong, disciplined, and do not take any shortcuts in life, but somehow, you need to learn to loosen up a little, become more humorous, and enjoy life to the fullest.

THE MALE OX

The male Ox usually has a great appetite and takes pleasure from the material things in life. He also has a love for nature and enjoys homemade food. Prudent and practical, you will hardly ever see an Ox man on a shopping spree. A real conservative at heart, he does not appreciate novelties or changes and prefers to keep everything the way it is. A male Ox is very organized, so his room must be neat and systematic, but only he will understand it.

Other qualities of the male Ox are his sincerity and loyalty. To him, honor and responsibility are everything, and he takes his duty seriously. Hardworking and diligent, he is well-known for his patience and persistence. He is rarely indecisive or impulsive; in fact, he is very cautious in everything he does and insists on keeping his feet firmly on the ground. Never a dreamer like the Sheep or an adventurer like the Tiger, the male Ox prefers a stable life and prefers to plan ahead for the future.

Not the talkative type, the male Ox is often quiet in a crowd, and he does not readily show his emotion. Among all his acquaintances, there are only a handful he trusts. Careful and serious, he is not as popular as the Dragon or the Monkey. But with his intelligence and talents, even though he does not really want to be in the spotlight, many times he becomes the leader within a group. However, although he appears confident, underneath the surface he is a pessimist and constantly doubts himself.

Protective and proud, he refuses to show his weakness and reveal his true self to most people. Thus, the male Ox can be extremely difficult to understand, even to his dear friends or family. But, realistically, if you are in an Ox's circle of friends, you should brace yourself for a true and devoted lifelong friendship.

A deep thinker and a philosopher, the male Ox is not particularly quick-witted. He is also stubborn to a fault, and he knows it. Once he has made up his mind, no one and nothing can sway him. Sometimes, his belief will turn into an obsession or a fetish. And if this extreme belief is combined with the male Ox's destructive, authoritative and military-like manner, you will find men such as Adolf Hitler or Napoleon Bonaparte.

A dutiful and disciplined man, who appears cold at times, the male Ox is immune to public opinion. He always chooses to do things on his own terms at his own pace. He is ambitious but does not lose sight of reality.

Eventually, he will slowly climb to the top. In most cases, he is too honorable to take any shortcuts and too cautious to take any risky opportunity. Instead, he favors doing things step by step, and that is also how he earns his success ultimately.

In relationships, the male Ox is not particularly romantic. Inhibited and conservative, do not expect him to give his partner a candlelight dinner by the beach or dozens of long-stem roses at work, or even gently whisper sweet words. That is just too much to ask a male Ox. There is a famous Chinese idiom about a man playing a lute to a cow, implying he is wasting his breath on the wrong audience. The male Ox believes actions speak louder than words and prefers to show his affection through his actions.

In order to find happiness in life, the male Ox must learn to be less gloomy and biased, throw away his dogmatic and dull personality, and lighten up a bit to enjoy the humorous and the fun in life.

THE FEMALE OX

Compared to the male Ox, the determined and reliable female Ox is definitely more outspoken. It could be said that she is quite eloquent. If you try to debate with this articulate Ox female, nine out of ten times you will surrender to her persuasive skills. It is evident by the way she talks and the way she walks that the female Ox is strong-willed and authoritative. At the same time, she is dependable, calm and methodical. Margaret Thatcher and Princess Diana are two famous Ox women.

Generally fair-minded and a great listener, she is a

devoted and caring friend who is popular among her small circle of friends. It is not fair to say that she has no friends, it is just that she values only the handful that are closest to her heart. Although extremely loyal to her friends and family, she is still a very private person, resenting anyone who tries to pry into her personal life. Also, she can be strongly biased and prejudiced, many times judging people quickly and capable of instantly labeling individuals as liked or disliked. Moreover, underneath her apparent friendliness lies an agitated bull that is fearsome and explosive when crossed. In fact, she will never forgive those who betray her. And with the female Ox's exceptional memory, it is also very unlikely that she will forget any deception throughout her life.

Dignified and dexterous, she is too proud to take any shortcuts in life. To her, success ought to be earned, not given. Industrious and precise, she always plans ahead and has goals for herself. A born traditionalist, the female Ox often abides by the law and will make a stand when she sees unfairness. Interestingly, though, she herself is never a bully; instead, in many cases all of her friends must gather around to stop her from going after those who bully others.

Her home is very important to her and she sees it as her sanctuary. It is not necessarily luxurious or fancy, but it must be comfortable. The female Ox prefers to live in rural areas to be close to nature. If unable to live in the country, a garden or a house near the water can also bring pleasure to the nature-loving Ox woman.

Loyal and practical, the female Ox is the typical ideal wife. She knows how to take care of her husband and children and is always neat and punctual. Steadfast and protective, this no-nonsense type of girl is not particularly romantic, but she certainly carries more than her share of the load.

In affairs of the heart, the Ox woman can be terribly naïve and inflexible. She has high standards, which she not only applies to herself, but insists her partner abide by as well. Her naïveté may be a reason that younger men can often woo her. In the event of a broken heart, she has the tendency to grieve far too long, refusing to move on.

A good lesson for the female Ox is to try to overcome her judgmental nature and learn to be flexible and open up more to others.

OX AT WORK

Born leaders, Ox people are dependable and trustworthy. They are careful and dexterous, and know how to achieve their goals step by step. Always keeping their feet firmly on the ground, they never lose sight of reality.

Their reputation means more to them than wealth. And, they are usually born with an innate ability to achieve great things. Aristotle, Malcolm X, and Walt Disney are just three Ox people who have made their names and marks in history. Determined and industrious, most Ox people can achieve success in their chosen professions through diligence and hard work.

As a boss, the Ox can be extremely authoritative. This creature enjoys being in power and giving orders. Therefore, they can be difficult at times because they tend to listen to no one but themselves. Ox people come across as being strong believers in themselves and never regret any decision they have made. And when in power, the Ox sometimes tends to lose their temper, perhaps causing problems in the company. Fortunately, the Ox will not set any unreasonable goal for their staff.

As a partner, the Ox is organized and systematic. They are practical and will not be happy unless everything is done by the book. They can be difficult to communicate with because they don't reveal how they think or feel, but even if it takes a long time to get an Ox to open up, it is worth it. The Ox needs a creative and more open-minded counterpart to balance the partnership. And when in negotiations, the Ox can play the bad cop while the partner plays the good cop.

As a colleague, the Ox is friendly and devoted. They like to serve and help people and are born problem-solvers. In fact, if you are in trouble, call up your Ox friend and he or she will patiently listen to your two-hour-long story before giving you any of his or her precious advice.

BEST OX OCCUPATIONS

Architect	Judge
Banker	Landlord
Composer	Police or military
Cook or chef	officer
Doctor	Religious leader
Estate manager	Soldier
Farmer	Teacher
Gardener	Technician
Insurance broker	

FAMOUS OX

Adolf Hitler	Margaret Thatcher
Anthony Hopkins	Meg Ryan
Aristotle	Meryl Streep
Bill Cosby	Napoleon Bonaparte
Charles Chaplin	Paul Newman
Clark Gable	Princess Diana
Dustin Hoffman	Robert Redford
George Clooney	Saddam Hussein
Jack Nicholson	Vincent Van Gogh
Jim Carrey	Walt Disney
Malcolm X	Warren Beatty

COMPATIBILITY

The Chinese believe each animal sign is most compatible with signs that are four years apart, and least compatible with the sign that is six years apart. Based on this concept, a circle can be drawn with all signs, locating the Triangle of Affinity and the Circle of Conflict.

TRIANGLE OF AFFINITY
Ox, Snake, Rooster are the Triangle of Affinity

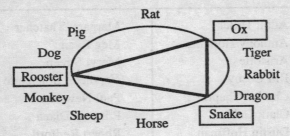

CIRCLE OF CONFLICT
Ox's conflict sign is Sheep

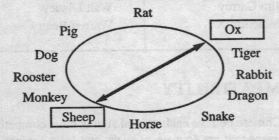

Signs	Rating 1–10	Relationship
Ox with Rat	8	A very good match
Ox with Ox	7	Conservative! Mutually protect and provide
Ox with Tiger	6	Difficult but possible
Ox with Rabbit	6	Not a balanced relationship
Ox with Dragon	5	Don't, the two of you will fight constantly

Ox with Snake	8	This union can be a good one
Ox with Horse	5	Unfortunately, they will part
Ox with Sheep	*4*	*Better stay away*
Ox with Monkey	8	Nice—they are compatible and stable
Ox with Rooster	8	You are lucky to find each other
Ox with Dog	5	This is one rocky relationship
Ox with Pig	6	Why not—it's worth a try

Ox with Rat   8
A very good match

Although these two signs appear to have little in common, this will be an excellent and loving relationship. The Rat and the Ox share mutual love and understanding. The Rat will admire the Ox as a devoted partner, and the Ox will be attracted to the outspoken and intelligent Rat. They will be very sympathetic and compassionate to each other and both will be enriched. The Rat, being the more aggressive one, does not seem to mind the slow pace of the serious and diligent Ox. They can be great not only as lovers but also as partners. Lucky you to find each other!

Ox with Ox   7
Conservative! Mutually protect and provide

This is a solid and stable relationship. Both people are hardworking and diligent. Although the Ox naturally wants to dominate, fortunately, these two will try to avoid conflict and find ways to balance power. Both dutiful and inflexible, the Ox has the tendency to be too serious; so the Ox-Ox combination might create a couple who are all work and no play. Money will be comfortable because of this. And these two like-minded thinkers are not good at communication. While they protect and provide for each other, they do not share a deep understanding. Each party should learn to loosen up a little and share thoughts and feelings with each other.

Ox with Tiger 6
Difficult but possible

This duo is in for quite a relationship. The Ox and the Tiger are both stubborn and determined, so they can start fighting for the smallest, most meaningless reason. The Ox is not known for having a great sense of humor, so the playful Tiger may find it hard to share thoughts and jokes with the Ox. When there is a problem, the Ox might try to be tolerant and hope the problem will go away, but the demanding Tiger will not hesitate to confront the Ox. This relationship is difficult, but still possible if the Ox learns to be more flexible and brings the Tiger under control.

Ox with Rabbit 6
Not a balanced relationship

These two will enjoy a peaceful and harmonious life. The Rabbit seeks security and that is exactly what the Ox can provide. Nevertheless, this will not be a balanced relationship. The Rabbit will feel the Ox is being condescending. The refined Rabbit is indulgent and sometimes can be self-centered, but the hardworking Ox is enduring and unaware of the needs of the sentimental Rabbit. At the same time, the Rabbit will find the Ox too inflexible and pessimistic. Though there will be no fiery quarrels between these two, a cold war and silent resignation will exist when they have problems.

Ox with Dragon 5
Don't, the two of you will fight constantly

When you put a powerful and dominant Dragon together with an inflexible and stubborn Ox, you get a constantly fighting combination. Being the practical one in the relationship, the Ox likes to stick by the rules and follow daily routines. On the contrary, the willful Dragon does not like to play by the rules and is idealistic and unpractical about the future. They often fight for dominance and each tends to believe only his or her way is the right way. They do have strong physical attraction, but the relationship might not be long-lived.

Ox with Snake 8
This union can be a good one

Finally, the Ox finds an equal partner in the Ox-Snake relationship. This will be a long and lasting partnership because each can respect and share with the other. The dependent Ox will give the ambitious Snake all the support they need. And the Snake will have a stronger influence over the Ox than the other way around. However, the Ox will not mind a bit because the Ox enjoys feeling needed by the Snake. Both are practical planners, enjoying working toward their long-term goals.

Ox with Horse   5
Unfortunately, they will part

The Ox and the Horse move at different paces and often
think in different directions. The conventional Ox is cautious and likes to play by the rules, whereas the wild
Horse prefers to be impulsive and risky. The irresponsible
and adventurous nature of the Horse can really drive the
patient Ox crazy, and eventually the Ox will walk away
from the relationship. Both are lousy at communication,
yet both are anxious to lead. When things don't go the
way they want, each tends to blame the other for the
failure. This will not be a long-lasting relationship.

Ox with Sheep   4
Better stay away

Being six years apart from the Ox makes the Sheep the
conflicted opposite of the Ox. Needless to say, these two
have absolutely nothing in common. The Ox is stubborn
and punctual while the Sheep is laid-back and can't keep
track of time. The Ox is disciplined, which can be beneficial to the sloppy and disorganized Sheep. But eventually, the Ox will become tired of taking care of the mess
left by the Sheep all the time and will call it quits. Although some may say opposites attract, these two just
don't see eye to eye.

Ox with Monkey   8
Nice—they are compatible and stable

Even the serious Ox cannot resist the charm of the creative and cheerful Monkey. One might think the Ox

probably couldn't tolerate the adventurous Monkey (like Ox with the impulsive Horse) but surprisingly, the Ox finds the Monkey's sparkling personality fascinating. In fact, the naughty Monkey enjoys teasing the serious Ox, but often with tenderness and love. This helps the disciplined Ox to loosen up a little bit and become more open-minded. These two may have some misunderstandings occasionally, but the optimistic Monkey knows just the right way to resolve it and eventually cheer up the Ox.

Ox with Rooster   8
You are lucky to find each other

Luckily, the relationship between the Ox and the Rooster will be harmonious and stable. Indeed, this combination might be the best match for the Ox. Both signs are well organized and like to plan ahead, and both care a lot about money and financial security. Between the two, the Rooster probably will be the spokesperson for this couple, and the Ox enjoys watching the Rooster show off. They are very compatible, and both will benefit from the other's company. Occasionally, the opinionated Rooster should learn to tone down the attitude and resolve the differences.

Ox with Dog   5
This is one rocky relationship

These two don't have much in common, and the Dog might suffer in this Ox-Dog union. As both are loyal and hardworking, these two seem similar at first glance, but the truth is that they can start a battle over the silliest topic. The witty Dog will criticize the serious Ox for lacking a sense of a humor, and the practical Ox will complain about the charitable Dog's unrealistic desire to save the world. The Ox will be counting every dime, saving up for the rainy days, while the Dog tries to persuade the Ox to donate some for a better cause. This is a couple with a rocky start and a lot to overcome.

Ox with Pig   **6**
Why not—it's worth a try

The Ox-Pig combination can be interesting. The disciplined Ox will most likely be the one that takes control in the duo. After all, the easygoing Pig will probably be busy hanging out with friends instead of spending time at a desk filing a tax report. It is no surprise to learn that the Ox enjoys staying in on a beautiful Sunday morning, reading a nice book or simply just sleeping in. On the contrary, the Pig will start calling up every single friend to arrange a picnic by the lake or all-night dancing at a nightclub. But, despite the differences, this partnership definitely deserves a chance to succeed.

THE FIVE ELEMENTS:
The Ox—the natural element is Water

THE METAL OX: 1901, 1961, 2021

Most Ox are hardworking and stubborn, and the Metal element strengthens these qualities even more. Resourceful and self-sufficient, the Metal Ox can become a one-man army when he is obsessed with achieving his goals. In fact, they can work around the clock for days just to get things done, refusing to accept the word "failure." This type of Ox is not very affectionate but is still capable of being fanatical about classical music. They are famous for being persons of few words, but their strong sense of responsibility makes it easy to rely on their words. On the negative side, the Metal Ox is arrogant, and can be narrow-minded and domineering.

THE WATER OX: 1853, 1913, 1973

The Water element makes the Ox more realistic and practical even among other Ox. Water brings sensitivity to the Ox and enables them to listen and help others. More open to suggestion, the Water Ox is less stubborn compared to Ox of other elements and will not be upset if asked to compromise.

The Water Ox is hardworking and patient. Because their natural element is Water, the double-Water element somehow slows them down but also makes them flexible. They can concentrate on more than one goal at a time, and will eventually make their mark in their careers and professions. On the downside, the Water Ox is not too tolerant with individuals who are self-pitying and weak.

THE WOOD OX: 1865, 1925, 1985

When combined with the Ox's natural Water element, the Wood Ox blossoms and grows. This Water-Wood combination makes the Wood Ox the most creative and innovative type of Ox. Less rigid than others of his sign, the Wood Ox is blessed with a good sense of humor, physical strength, and natural energy. The Wood element also makes the Ox sociable. Diligent, open-minded, and even witty at times, the Wood Ox is capable of teamwork and great accomplishment.

THE FIRE OX: 1877, 1937, 1997

The conflicting combination of Fire and Water produces an impatient Fire Ox. Lacking most of the typical Ox personality traits, the Fire Ox is usually forceful, and aggressive. Although most Ox consider themselves superior to others, they usually don't show their arrogance. The Fire Ox, on the other hand, wave their royal flag around and announce to the world their belief in their superiority. No wonder the Fire Ox often offends people. Despite their lack of diplomacy, the Fire Ox is normally honest and fair, and does try to avoid unnecessary conflicts. In general, the Fire Ox is very protective toward the ones they love but needs to learn to be more diplomatic.

THE EARTH OX: 1889, 1949, 2009

The Earth element possesses many of the Ox qualities such as—patience, tranquillity and reliability. So the combination of the Water-Earth Ox makes them enduring and the least creative type of all Ox. They are always faithful to their duty, and understand their own limitations. Constantly seeking security, the Earth Ox is not interested in adventure or risky investment. Although not sensitive enough to others, the Earth Ox are extremely loyal to their own principles and the people they love. Determined and enduring, this Ox may move slowly, but eventually he will go far.

The Powerful Tiger

Ranking order   **Third**

YEARS			ELEMENTS
1902 Feb.08	–	1903 Jan.28	Water
1914 Jan.26	–	1915 Feb.13	Wood
1926 Feb.13	–	1927 Feb.01	Fire
1938 Jan.31	–	1939 Feb.18	Earth
1950 Feb.17	–	1951 Feb.05	Metal
1962 Feb.05	–	1963 Jan.24	Water
1974 Jan.23	–	1975 Feb.10	Wood
1986 Feb.09	–	1987 Jan.28	Fire
1998 Jan.28	–	1999 Feb.05	Earth
2010 Feb.14	–	2011 Feb.02	Metal
2022 Feb.01	–	2023 Jan.21	Water

Force:	**Yang**
Natural element:	**Wood**
Season and principal month:	**Winter—February**
Direction of its sign:	**Northeast 60–East 30 degrees**
Hours ruled by:	**3 A.M.–5 A.M.**
Best companions:	**Horse, Dog**
Worst companions:	**Snake, Monkey**
Color:	**Orange, Dark Gold**

PERSONALITY CHARACTERISTICS

Positive	Negative
Ambitious	Aggressive
Brave	Arrogant
Confident	Critical
Determined	Demanding
Dynamic	Disobedient
Engaging	Domineering
Enthusiastic	Hotheaded
Generous	Impatient
Hardworking	Moody
Honorable	Quarrelsome
Idealistic	Reckless
Independent	Selfish
Lovable	Stubborn
Loyal	Suspicious
Open-minded	Vain
Optimistic	
Respectful	
Thoughtful	
Warmhearted	
Wise	

TIGER—THE ANIMAL

In China, Tigers symbolize power, vigor, dignity, bravery, and leadership. Tigers may not be the kings of the jungle, but they have been deeply rooted in Chinese religion and folklore for centuries. In fact, they are so highly regarded that Tigers sometimes appear to have almost magical powers. To this day, images of Dragons and Tigers are often paired off on walls of temples, and in some suburban areas in China and Taiwan, a statue of the "Master Tiger" is also placed under the altar and worshiped by thousands of followers. Gamblers and people in show business believe that worshiping the Master Tiger will bring them fame and fortune.

Sometimes, however, Tigers can also be seen as symbols of evil, violence, and danger. This is probably because in ancient China, Tigers would often come out of the woods and terrorize small villages. Many folk tales praised the heroes who were brave enough to fight with the Tigers. Amongst Chinese folk heroes, Wu Song became probably one of the most famous ones after he eventually saved his village by battling with a Tiger barehanded.

Over the centuries, it has become a custom to hang a good-luck Tiger ornament on boats during the Dragon Boat Festival. Also on this day, children will often wear an ornamental look-alike amulet around their necks to protect them from evil.

TIGER PEOPLE

"Born leader" is the key phrase for Tigers. Born under the sign of courage, you are quick-witted and alert, energetic and independent, courageous and powerful. It is no wonder people will faithfully and confidently follow you.

You adore challenges and competitions. Admit it, you often take risks even when you don't have to. Tempting danger thrills you, and you're hungry for adventures. However, owing to your tendency to be too impulsive, it may not always be wise to follow you. You can be extremely rebellious against any petty authority; after all, you'd rather give orders than take them.

Perhaps this is why you are most likely to be the one to cry out, "Let's Go!" You have all the qualities required to become a great leader or a rebel. You are outspoken and critical on issues, and you don't back down when facing obstacles. You are a daring fighter, capable of standing up to the bitter end for what you believe is right, and you are not afraid to speak up loud and clear about what's on your mind. Truly, you would make a fine revolutionary.

Tigers are very confident, perhaps overly so sometimes. You love adventures, and are addicted to excitement. You are the type of person who will risk it all just to get what you want, even if it is only a competition. You expect to be obeyed and not the other way around, and it is better not to challenge your authority because whoever disobeys you will become the object of the Tiger's furious quick temper.

However, noble and fearless Tiger people are well respected for their courage; even by those working against them. You are independent and confident, and seldom ask anyone for help. On the surface, you often seem calm and in control, but deep down, there is always some hidden aggressiveness. But don't take that the wrong way, Tigers are not predators who get what they want by crushing others. In fact, you are warm, sincere, honorable and humorous. Although you can be selfish from time to time about the little things, you are capable of great generosity.

There will never be a dull moment with a Tiger. You

are playful and unpredictable, daring and reckless. Always hating to be ignored, you love the spotlight and crave attention, and you are always tense and seem to revel in being in a hurry. You love to try new cuisine, go to new places, and be adventurous and explore new things. If you are in his circle of friends, you will have fun new experiences and the Tiger will try his best to protect you.

It is not easy to resist a Tiger, for you are a very magnetic character. In fact, you walk and talk in such an assertive and powerful way that authority seems natural to you. You are impetuous yet serene, compassionate yet fearsome, a person of great strength and ability. Time and time again, people are awed and mesmerized by you.

Because you are always in a hurry to get things done right, you usually choose to operate alone. You like to work, moreover, you are hardworking and dynamic. If someone assigns a task to you, the job will be undertaken and accomplished with enthusiasm and efficiency. But money doesn't directly interest or motivate you. Still, Tigers need not worry about money, because they are also fortunate animals; just when you fear the money is gone, more seems to show up.

In general, Tigers are quite impatient and usually not the sit-and-wait types. You jump into action and sometimes regret it afterward. Imaginative and fun-loving, you are often attracted by babies and animals. Reputation and image mean a great deal to you, and you try hard to maintain a certain image of authority and dignity. Tiger people are sensitive and emotional. You are capable of great love, you often become too intense about it. You are also territorial and possessive; when in an argument, you always expect your friends to take your side. And because you are simply so adorable and irresistible, most of the time, your friends will. Though sensitive and sentimental, your dramatic mood swings can still turn you into a nasty and mean bully when you are provoked. Therefore, it is better not to rub any Tiger the wrong way, as the Tiger can be extremely dangerous and will go to any lengths to get revenge, even if it means bringing himself down with you. Generally suspicious, you do not trust people easily.

Life with a Tiger is bound to be a colorful, volatile roller-coaster ride. It will be filled with joy, laughter, tears, and despair. You are generally optimistic, but if you sink into a depression, it will be extremely hard to pull you out of it. As a lover, you are passionate and romantic, but the real challenge for you is to grasp the true meaning of moderation.

THE MALE TIGER

"Born to lead rather than to obey" is his motto, and he takes orders from no one. Strong and powerful, the male Tiger is one energetic fellow. Never intimidated by any authority, and not afraid to voice his opinion, the male Tiger grew up as his group's spokesperson. He seeks attention wherever he goes, but he often gets noticed without even trying.

He is the kind of young guy every father with a daughter fears. After all, he is the typical bad boy that women seem to fall for, and this Mr. Tiger is brave, confident, daring, and noble. He is probably the honorable prince who comes to rescue the princess in the fairy tale. He detests petty authority and feels extremely protective toward his loved ones. Leonardo DiCaprio and Tom Cruise are two famous Tiger men.

The male Tiger has a good heart and can be very generous and compassionate. He will also be a smart and elegant dresser as well as well mannered and thoughtful. He also stands by his friends when they need him the most. Most Tiger men appear peaceful on the outside; underneath, they are some passionate and aggressive creatures.

He is idealistic, tending to see things his own way instead of the normal logical way. And many times, this idealism mixed with his adventurous and reckless character might lead him to an unexpected downfall. This can be dangerous since he has an incredibly big ego and his overconfidence sometimes means that he can't take failure gracefully. So, it is always wise not to provoke a Tiger, especially a wounded one.

Also, because he is so intense and impulsive, he is bound to experience mood swings. And when the outburst starts, bystanders better start looking for cover. The male Tiger does not hide his emotions; instead, he wants the whole world to know about his frustration. A beaten Tiger does not need your sympathy, but he wants you to be there to listen to his complaint about the injustice. He will feel the world has been unfair to him, and he waits for everyone around him to comfort and encourage him. Fortunately, a male Tiger is optimistic as well. Usually he will quickly get over it and forget all about the defeat and move on to his next grand plan and challenge.

As lovers, male Tigers will be loyal and passionate, never boring. He is thoughtful and lovable and his imagination and impulsiveness often lead to surprising his partners with romantic getaways or dances in the moonlight. Although his roller-coaster-quick temper might be a problem sometimes, it usually vanishes quickly just as it comes without warning. If you are involved with an unpredictable Tiger man, just sit back and enjoy the ride.

THE FEMALE TIGER

Tiger women are usually beautiful and alluring. Strong and intelligent, sexy and exciting, they are the dream of many young men. Actually, female Tigers are famous for their charisma and beauty. One famous Tiger lady was Marilyn Monroe. As America's twentieth-century sex symbol, she certainly had the power to attract guys like moths flying toward the light.

Daring and strong, the female Tiger is intense in her feelings of love and takes family and friends seriously. Always sought after by young men, she will have numerous love affairs. But she loves children and tends to have several of them, and she instinctively knows how to play and communicate with children.

Always trying to be honest and frank in her opinions of others, Tiger women do not know and or care when or if they should be quiet. She is fair, noble and will not give up a good fight for a good cause. Even though she dislikes authority, she tends to be very authoritarian and often bosses around those who work with her.

When all these characteristic traits are put together the image of the female Tiger comes into focus. Someone who is outspoken, independent, intelligent, and bossy. Attractive and smart, authoritative and candid, when she needs to twist someone's arm to get what she wants, she does not feel remorse or guilt. She is frank, honest, never wastes time beating around the bush, and likes to be in control. A daring dresser who follows no fashion rules but her own, Tiger woman dresses and lives with great style.

With her talents and determination, Tiger lady often succeeds at a young age. She loves to live an adventurous life and does not like to plan ahead. Ambitious as she is, she can probably start her own business. Even though money is not all she cares about, with the luck she was born with, Tiger lady does not need to worry about money throughout her life.

She never changes, not because she can't, but because she doesn't think she needs to. Nevertheless, the female Tiger should learn to be less predatory and stubborn, less arrogant and critical; she must learn to master the art of self-control in order to have a more smooth and successful life.

TIGER AT WORK

Tigers are formidable business leaders. No challenge is too big or too small for a Tiger. After all, a challenge is a challenge, and Tigers will go to any lengths just to prove they can do it. Tiger people are aggressive and ambitious when it comes to their careers.

Tigers are dreamers, generally full of moneymaking ideas. However, they have a tendency to jump into action before they spend adequate time planning. Once a Tiger sets his goal, he always goes for it with full force; however, his impulsive personality may lure him to something else, and Tigers will detour from their original goal to another one. However, in spite of these detours, it usually does not take long for Tigers to work their way up the ranks to the top. After all, they are born to lead and are very capable and determined to succeed.

As a boss, Tigers are quite popular and generally well respected among their staff. But since most Tigers don't hide their emotions well, Tiger bosses show their likes and dislikes, and their favorites tend to get better treatment and promotions than the rest. But even though everyone notices this, no one dares to complain, because at times, Tiger bosses can be fearsome. However, mostly they are generous and open-minded and will be able to create a fun, creative working environment.

As a business partner, the Tiger can be quite unpredictable and impulsive. Planning ahead and applying logic do not mean much to them and therefore, they need to partner with someone who is detailed and organized. As the partner of a Tiger, you must learn to think what they think and stop them from acting too quickly. In general, they need someone to hold their hand and persuade them when they become unfocused.

As a colleague, the Tiger is fun to be around. They are liked for their generosity and warm hearts. Marilyn Monroe and Jodie Foster are two other famous Tiger people.

BEST TIGER OCCUPATIONS

Advertising executive	Musician
Athlete	Police officer
Chairman	Politician
Designer	Publicist
Entrepreneur	Rebel leader
Explorer	Stockbroker
Film star	Stunt person
Film/theater director	Teacher
Head of state	Trade union leader
Lion tamer	Writer/poet
Military officer	

FAMOUS TIGERS

Dwight D. Eisenhower	Queen Elizabeth II
Jodie Foster	Rosie O'Donnell
Karl Marx	Stevie Wonder
Leonardo DiCaprio	Sun Yat-sen
Ludwig von Beethoven	Tom Cruise
Marco Polo	William Wordsworth
Marilyn Monroe	

COMPATIBILITY

The Chinese believe each animal sign is most compatible with signs that are four years apart, and least compatible with the sign that is six years apart. Based on this concept a circle can be drawn with all signs, locating the Triangle of Affinity and the Circle of Conflict.

TRIANGLE OF AFFINITY

Tiger, Horse, Dog are the Triangle of Affinity

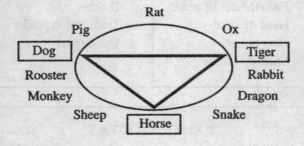

CIRCLE OF CONFLICT

Tiger's conflict sign is Monkey

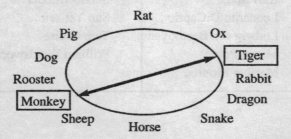

Signs	Rating 1–10	Relationship
Tiger with Rat	7	In order to succeed, both must endure
Tiger with Ox	6	Difficult but possible
Tiger with Tiger	5	Two Tigers—not recommended
Tiger with Rabbit	6	Only if they share the same interests
Tiger with Dragon	7	Despite minor difficulties it's good for marriage
Tiger with Snake	4	Difficult to know what they see in each other
Tiger with Horse	8	Why not, they have lots in common
Tiger with Sheep	2	One of the worst combinations
Tiger with Monkey	*3*	*Better stay away from each other*
Tiger with Rooster	6	Not a balanced relationship
Tiger with Dog	8	Good, a balanced and harmonic relationship
Tiger with Pig	7	They are very different but this will work

Tiger with Rat   **7**
In order to succeed both must endure

When they first see each other, it is love at first sight. The Tiger is attracted to the Rat's charm and liveliness while the Rat finds the Tiger alluring and lovable. But after the first spark of love fades, their relationship will turn into constant minor skirmishes. Both possess quick tempers and stubborn personalities, and both are too proud to compromise. Nevertheless, this relationship can still succeed if they both make efforts to communicate and learn to agree about their differences. In general, there is still hope for a long, loving marriage for these two.

Tiger with Ox   6
Difficult but possible

This duo is in for quite a tempestuous relationship. The Ox and Tiger are both stubborn and determined, so they can start fighting with each other for the smallest and most meaningless reason. The Ox is not famous for having a great sense of humor, and the playful Tiger finds it hard to share thoughts and jokes with the Ox. When there is a problem, the Ox might try to be tolerant and hope the problem will go away, but the demanding Tiger will not hesitate to confront the Ox. This relationship is difficult, but still possible if the Ox learns to be more open-minded and authoritative so the Tiger can be brought under control.

Tiger with Tiger   5
Two Tigers—not recommended

The combination of two Tigers can be very tricky. On good days, these two will enjoy a passionate and wild relationship, full of fun and impulsive excitement; they believe in love at first sight and share laughter and jokes together. But on bad days, these two simply can't see eye to eye. They are extremely competitive and seem ready to jump on each other and start a fiery fight. Have you ever watched two Tigers fighting over a lamb chop on the Discovery Channel? Then you've got the picture. The Tiger craves the limelight; therefore, these two will be constantly competing to be the center of attention.

Tiger with Rabbit   6
Only if they share the same interests

The partnership between the Tiger and the Rabbit can be difficult at times, but basically, these two are both witty and understand how to get along. The suave Rabbit is smart enough to let the Tiger take the lead; at least, the Rabbit lets the Tiger believe that. In fact, the Rabbit knows just how to manipulate the Tiger to get things done. And, Tigers occasionally show their true colors by trying to dominate or bully the sensitive Rabbit. In order to make this relationship work, the couple must share some interests.

Tiger with Dragon   7
Despite minor difficulties, it's good for marriage

A relationship between the Tiger and the Dragon will never be boring. Both are powerful and highly motivated, and both are passionate and action-oriented. Together, these two are quite a match because they are equally talented and demanding, and neither of them is intimidated by the other. The Dragon provides a strong influence on the Tiger; however, the Tiger has better business sense. Similar in temperament, they actually understand each other better than predicted, and since they are both frank and straightforward, they won't shy away from talking about their problems.

Tiger with Snake   **4**
Difficult to know what they see in each other

The combination of the Tiger and the Snake will be a difficult one, as these two don't have much in common and they approach life from very different angles and perspectives. The dramatic Tiger is more outspoken than the Snake, and likes to follow gut feelings instead of the head. On the contrary, the secretive Snake is always suspicious of everyone, including the Tiger, and prefers to organize things in a more systematic way. There will be conflicts between the two owing to some misunderstandings.

Tiger with Horse   **8**
Why not—they have lots in common

Finally, here is a couple that shares much in common and enjoys each other's company. Both the Tiger and the Horse are impulsive, and they are definitely not the type to wait. In fact, they are somewhat impatient, so they usually jump right into the things they are passionate about. Although at times, they will still fight like a normal couple, they know each other too well for quarrels to last very long. Better yet, the Horse always knows how to tame and comfort a Tiger in a depression. Both parties will benefit a great deal from this partnership.

Tiger with Sheep   **2**
One of the worst combinations

There is a famous Chinese saying about sending a Sheep directly to a Tiger, which implies a situation that is doomed or suicidal. After all, as soon as the Tiger sees the

Sheep, he will not hesitate to attack and devour this poor animal. This is probably why most Chinese believe the Tiger-Sheep combination is one of the worst combinations. The soft and indecisive Sheep will be controlled and manipulated by the bossy Tiger. And the laid-back nature of the Sheep will probably drive the impatient and impulsive Tiger crazy. If these two form a family, the somewhat lazy Sheep will refuse to do the dishes and the aggressive Tiger will not pick up the housework. These two just don't want to compromise.

Tiger with Monkey 3
Better stay away from each other

Tiger and Monkey are both competitive and refuse to compromise. Both proud and intelligent, the Tiger may be easily offended by the Monkey's remarks or comments, while the Monkey may not have the patience for the Tiger's explosive temper. These two will fight and retaliate at each other, and will always be on guard for the next possible provocation. Tiger, which is six years apart from Monkey, is the sign of conflict for the Monkey. What more can be said, except that you two are definitely not meant for each other?

Tiger with Rooster 6
Not a balanced relationship

Although the relationship between the Tiger and the Rooster first appears promising, because they share many things in common, the truth is, it will go downhill soon afterward. Roosters, as perfectionists, have the tendency to order others to follow their rules. This lecturing nature of Rooster will annoy the independent Tiger and bring out the worst of the Tiger's rebellious personality. In general, this is not a balanced relationship. They both have the inclination to pick on the other for his or her faults. Misunderstanding might be one of the biggest issues they have to overcome. But if they share some common interests, they might be able to find ways to patch things up.

Tiger with Dog   8
Good, a balanced and harmonic relationship

Both perfectionists, the Tiger and the Dog actually seem to know a way to get along perfectly. The understanding Dog knows how to handle the impulsive and playful Tiger, and the Tiger appreciates the Dog's loyalty and good sense. Both are frank and sincere, and will not hide away from confronting problems between them. And best of all, these two signs will not hold grudges against each other and will not let one dominate. This will be a balanced and long-lasting relationship, and they will benefit from the partner's talents and experience.

Tiger with Pig   7
They are very different but this will work

When the Tiger and the Pig are in the same room, it means party time! These two are both party animals—sociable and popular. Worry-free and fun-loving, the Tiger and the Pig are both affectionate and gregarious. The combination of the Tiger and the Pig can be a good one because they can cooperate and support each other. They may appear different at first glance, but eventually, they will learn to appreciate each other and develop a better way to communicate.

THE FIVE ELEMENTS:
The Tiger—the natural element is Wood

THE METAL TIGER: 1890, 1950, 2010

The Metal Tiger is active and passionate. They often project an image of being outspoken and tough, and can be extremely bossy at times. The Metal Tiger can be very competitive when motivated. Full of confidence, they never doubt themselves and believe that they are capable of great things. Metal Tigers can succeed in any chosen profession because of their aggressive nature. Nevertheless, they should also learn to be flexible sometimes.

THE WATER TIGER: 1902, 1962, 2022

The Water element combined with the natural Wood element endows the Tiger with a calmer nature. Unlike the Tigers of other elements, the Water Tiger tends to be open-minded and sensitive and has the gift to see clearly and fairly. They see things objectively and this can teach them to relate to how others feel. These abilities make Water Tigers excellent judges.

THE WOOD TIGER: 1914, 1974, 2034

The double-Wood combination makes this Tiger emotional and charming. Always a party animal, the Wood Tiger is quite popular among peers and will enjoy an active social life. Nevertheless, underneath their friendliness, the Wood Tiger evaluates situations and is calculating about which circle of friends to enter. Their loyalty is mostly to themselves, and they tend to take the minimum responsibility possible. Most Tigers take criticism badly; the Wood Tiger is no exception. Wood Tigers should also learn to control their emotions better.

THE FIRE TIGER: 1866, 1926, 1986

The Fire Tiger is always on the run, ready for action, only caring about the present. "Seize the day" is one of their favorite mottoes, and Fire Tigers are animated yet changeable characters. They love to impress people with their vitality and optimistic personality. Nevertheless, they are also capable of an explosive temper. Fortunately, with this type of Tiger, their temper comes and goes easily and is never long-lasting. While Fire Tigers are brilliant leaders, they should also learn to relax and act less impulsively.

THE EARTH TIGER: 1878, 1938, 1998

The Earth Tiger is the quietest Tiger of them all. Responsible and fair, they tend not to judge or jump to any conclusion too quickly. The Earth element endowed these Tigers with a longer attention span, which enables them to focus on important tasks rather than being restless and impulsive. In the long run, Earth Tigers have the most potential to be successful because of their tranquil and responsible nature.

The Delicate Rabbit

Ranking order   **Fourth**

YEARS			ELEMENTS
1903 Jan.29	–	1904 Feb.15	Water
1915 Feb.14	–	1916 Feb.02	Wood
1927 Feb.02	–	1928 Jan.22	Fire
1939 Feb.19	–	1940 Feb.07	Earth
1951 Feb.06	–	1952 Jan.26	Metal
1963 Jan.25	–	1964 Feb.12	Water
1975 Feb.11	–	1976 Jan.30	Wood
1987 Jan.29	–	1988 Feb.16	Fire
1999 Feb.06	–	2000 Feb.04	Earth
2011 Feb.03	–	2012 Jan. 22	Metal
2023 Jan. 22	–	2024 Feb. 09	Water

Force:	Yin
Natural element:	Wood
Season and principal month:	Spring—March
Direction of its sign:	Direct East +30 and -30 degrees
Hours ruled by:	5A.M–7A.M
Best companions:	Sheep, Pig
Worst companions:	Rat, Dragon, Ox, Rooster
Color:	White

PERSONALITY CHARACTERISTICS

Positive	Negative
Affectionate	Complicated
Ambitious	Conformist
Artistic	Conservative
Considerate	Gossipy
Cultured	Hesitant
Diplomatic	Hypochondriac
Expressive	Indecisive
Honorable	Indifferent
Hospitable	Judgmental
Intelligent	Secretive
Moderate	Self-centered
Modest	Self-indulgent
Peaceful	Superficial
Popular	Timid
Principled	Touchy
Scholarly	
Sensitive	
Talented	
Virtuous	
Well mannered	

RABBIT—THE ANIMAL

The most famous Rabbit in Chinese culture is probably the "Jade Rabbit" who resides in the Moon Palace.

Legend has it that one day, three fairy sages transformed themselves into starving old beggars and bumped into a Fox, a Monkey, and a Rabbit. The sages asked these three animals for something to eat. The Fox and the Monkey both shared their food with the old men, but the poor Rabbit had nothing for itself or the sages. Determined to save the dying old men, the Rabbit jumped into a burning fire and offered itself to the beggars. The sages were so moved by the Rabbit's sacrifice that with their power they revived it and granted it eternal life. Then, the Rabbit was sent to live in the Moon Palace with Chang Er, the moon fairy.

Unlike Westerners, who associate the full moon with the myth of the werewolf, the Chinese are fascinated by the moon and celebrate Moon Festival, on the fifteenth day of the eighth lunar month, just like the West celebrates Christmas and Thanksgiving. This is the day for families to watch the full moon together, and enjoy moon cakes outdoors. It is also a romantic festival for lovers. Somehow, looking at the moon links them together.

Some people say that if you look closely at the moon, you will see the beautiful Chang Er fairy, and cheerful Jade Rabbit singing together in the Moon Palace.

RABBIT PEOPLE

The Rabbit is one of the most delicate among all twelve animals. You are usually kind and sweet and of course, popular. Nobody ignores you for you are good company and know exactly how to make the best of yourself.

A Rabbit's home is always beautiful because you are famous for your artistic sense and good taste. You are also well dressed. You love to throw lavish parties so you can show off your Beverly Hills mansion, and, of course, your spacious walk-in bedroom closet. Go on, open your closet, there will undoubtedly be many expensive and beautiful clothes inside.

Even though you are popular and loved by your friends and family, Rabbit people are pessimistic under the surface. You are conservative and insecure, explaining why you don't like changes. It is not easy to provoke calm Rabbit people. You don't like to argue, and you'd rather enjoy a quiet, peaceful life. You are also sentimental and compassionate. And yes, you cry easily, too. You will sob even from watching a Disney cartoon or when moved by a friend's personal problems. As a matter of fact, no one is a more compassionate listener than a Rabbit. You are sympathetic and truly soft at heart, which is why you are also voted as "the one who is most likely to open the door for a salesman." You are the answer to all salesmen's prayers, because nine out of ten Rabbit people will probably buy from the salesman at the door within five minutes.

Sometimes you appear unexceptional, but surprisingly, you often provoke extreme emotions. Some people adore you for your intelligence and suaveness, some see you as cunning or superficial. The truth is that probably you are quite a combination. You are mysterious yet practical, timid but ruthless when necessary.

You can be a great partner in a relationship. Romantic and sweet—faithful, too—Rabbit people never lack potential mates. The male Rabbit is somewhat picky and perhaps not a family man whereas the female Rabbit should probably spend less time admiring herself in the mirror and more time with friends.

Sometimes it is hard to decide whether to call you cautious or timid, because you will decide nothing before you have weighed the pros and cons from every angle. And that is probably why you do so well in your work. You are an excellent negotiator, and your natural suavity only adds to your skills. Sometimes you seem shy, but you always work well with people and achieve success in business. You know your own limits and are able to pace yourself to finish projects on time. You hate stressful situations and taking risks, and you definitely hate being forced to make a hasty decision. However, unless you abandon your conservative nature and become more aggressive, you will probably live a very normal and average life.

You are polite and gracious, and no one has such impeccable manners. Incapable of harsh words, you always try hard to keep the peace and make everyone happy. You are careful not to embarrass anyone in public, and you know just how to handle a sticky situation, which is probably why you hardly have any enemies.

You can be very affectionate and obliging, but only to the ones you love. Privacy is important to you, and you're reluctant to reveal things about yourself. You are very protective of your family and friends and also respect their privacy as much as your own. In fact, you never put your nose into someone else's business, believing that you are above prying and gossiping.

Even though you often compromise to avoid conflict, there is one thing you will not compromise—the quality of your life. You really know how to enjoy your life. Good wine, good food, expensive clothes, and stylish furniture are on your A-list. Vacation and routines are very important to you, too. If you go swimming every Tuesday night, you will probably keep that schedule for years and are unwilling to reschedule.

You always know how to get what you want even though this means manipulating others. And, you are able to achieve this without leaving a trace most of the time. Moreover, you are so skillful that no one will suspect that you have orchestrated everything.

When in peaceful or controlled circumstances, you will be relaxed and at ease, but any sudden change or conflict will make them unbalanced and turn you into a confused, sometimes even aggressive person. This is why Rabbits can be very unpredictable, with occasional mood swings that make them hard to understand. But you want to be in a controlled situation more than anything else.

At times, you can be really unreasonable, you are quite obsessed with security and your environment. You can be egocentric and picky on every little thing, sometimes making a big deal out of little things. A single drop of red wine on your carpet can drive you into hysteria. In general, you must learn to balance your nature, and try to see things from various angles.

THE MALE RABBIT

The male Rabbit always appears happy and content. He is sociable and popular. He is often well dressed and has perfect manners. Even though he always shows up looking his best, he is too individualistic to follow the latest fashion trends, preferring to dress himself the way he likes.

Imaginative and artistic, the male Rabbit has an eye for art and culture. He enjoys going to museums and admires great paintings, he is the kind of person who often watches the Discovery and National Geographic Channels to enrich his mind.

As a friend, he is a sympathetic listener. Yet do not expect him to rally for you and hold your hand through every single step of your hardship. He can be very compassionate, but lending his ears to listen to your problems is all he will do for you. He does not readily give advice, unless you directly ask him for it.

The male Rabbit seeks a peaceful and quiet life. He is not as adventurous as the Tiger, nor is he as aggressive as the Rat. On the contrary, any challenge to his stability and routine significantly disturbs him.

Home and family will be very important to him during his life. He is not really the family type; usually dating a lot before finally settling down. But the good news is, once he settles down, he will be a loving family man and will be faithful and extremely protective. Accordingly, the male Rabbit is very careful about money. He doesn't invest without doing the homework, and he only spends money when he thinks it is necessary. The exception to his money policy is the money spent on decorating his home. His home is his kingdom and the male Rabbit is extravagant when it comes to buying luxurious furniture.

As a hard worker and a faithful friend, the male Rabbit has a traditional outlook on life and doesn't like any changes.

THE FEMALE RABBIT

The female Rabbit is elegant and sophisticated. Appearance means a lot to her, which is why she spends a lot of time admiring herself in the mirror. Attractive and fun-loving, she is quite popular and is never short of suitors.

The Rabbit woman has a need for a material life, and is in no way stingy when it comes to her need and her home. She loves shopping with her friends and family, and is a natural at negotiation and bargaining. She is always stylishly dressed and places a great deal of value on the comfort of her home, often going the extra mile to find the exact piece of furniture. Nevertheless, the Rabbit woman can be extremely difficult and unbelievably stubborn sometimes. And a typical Rabbit woman tends to be particularly neat. For instance, while she worships her beautiful home and loves to invite people over to admire it, she can become hysterical when a drop of red wine is spilled, and will even count her spoons and forks after inviting guests over.

The female Rabbit has a great sense of humor and is good at giving practical advice. She can be a wonderful hostess, and whenever she is a guest at a party, she makes herself at home. She hates being alone and won't go to places or events without a friend or date.

This Rabbit woman can be emotional and hard to predict at times. But she knows just how to get things done the way she wants. Some call her cunning, some call her manipulative, but most of the time she is immune to criticism and indifferent to what others think of her. She can often avoid any conflict and confrontation with others through her diplomatic and well-mannered nature.

What she wants in her life is peace and comfort so she would never pursue an adventurous life like the Tiger woman. She does not commit easily and often agonizes over a relationship. Her dilemma is that while she can't stand being alone, she can't stand thoughts of settling down either. But her intuitive sense of timing will tell her when the time is right to settle down.

RABBIT AT WORK

Diplomatic and suave, Rabbit people are born great leaders and organizers. They are team players and will respect any group decision. After all, Rabbit people just want to make everyone happy, and they will try anything to keep it that way.

They have superb intuition, often seeing things before they happen, and are skilled at negotiation and bargaining. In addition, Rabbits have a sense of timing and know the right time to throw the punch to win the battle without anyone knowing a battle has been fought. While Rabbits are not particularly ambitious, their talents in dealing will bring them success in the trading business.

As a boss, the Rabbit loves team spirit and often expects the entire team to rally for the goal. They are not overly authoritative, but they expect you to foresee their wishes and needs. Rabbit bosses are easy to get along with and often have great success at recruiting the perfect person for a job. They are skilled managers but sometimes, to avoid conflict and confrontation at work, they can become too flexible in their efforts to please their team.

As a business partner, the Rabbit is intelligent and able. They have a conservative outlook on life, but their partner will have to convince them to take on risky business. Nevertheless, Rabbits are pros when it comes to negotiation and cannot be easily intimidated.

As a colleague, the Rabbit is a sincere and sympathetic listener and knows how to motivate their coworkers' spirits. And, they are fun to be around at the office Christmas party.

Generally speaking, with their great negotiation skills

and organizing mind, the Rabbits will do well in business. David Rockefeller and Albert Einstein are just two famous Rabbit people.

BEST RABBIT OCCUPATIONS

Accountant	Lawyer
Antique dealer	Librarian
Art collector	Pharmacist
Beautician	Politician
Chemist	Public relations
Diplomat	executive
Historian	Receptionist
Interior decorator	Tailor
Landlord	

FAMOUS RABBITS

Albert Einstein	Marie Curie
Bob Hope	Nicolas Cage
Brad Pitt	Queen Victoria
Confucius	Sting
Frank Sinatra	Tiger Woods
Ingrid Bergman	

COMPATIBILITY

The Chinese believe each animal sign is most compatible with signs that are four years apart, and least compatible with the sign that is six years apart. Based on this concept, a circle can be drawn with all signs, locating the Triangle of Affinity and the Circle of Conflict.

TRIANGLE OF AFFINITY
Rabbit, Pig, Sheep are the Triangle of Affinity

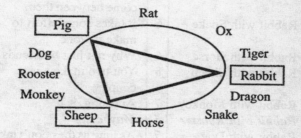

CIRCLE OF CONFLICT
Rabbit's conflict sign is Rooster

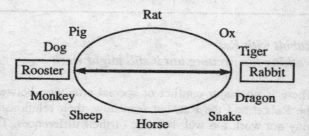

Signs	Rating 1–10	Relationship
Rabbit with Rat	6	Nothing too exciting, but it still might work
Rabbit with Ox	6	Not a balanced relationship
Rabbit with Tiger	6	Only if they share the same interest
Rabbit with Rabbit	7	Why not, as long as they have loads of money
Rabbit with Dragon	5	Their differences might come between them
Rabbit with Snake	6	It takes some effort to make it work
Rabbit with Horse	6	Why not just be friends
Rabbit with Sheep	8	You two make a nice couple
Rabbit with Monkey	7	Amusing
Rabbit with Rooster	*5*	*Maybe not*
Rabbit with Dog	7	As long as they don't take each other for granted
Rabbit with Pig	9	Very compatible, they will be happy together

Rabbit with Rat   *6*
Nothing too exciting but it still might work

There is no major conflict or special attraction between the Rabbit and the Rat, but somehow, their relationship may not work too well because of their differences. The

Rabbit can be oversensitive while the Rat is overcontrolling. Both have high expectations of each other, and this may cause problems between the two. This match may not seem to bring out the best in both personalities, but once joined, they will be difficult to separate. Basically, it will be an amicable relationship, and, in fact, sometimes these two make better business partners than lovers.

Rabbit with Ox   6
Not a balanced relationship

These two both enjoy a peaceful and harmonious life. The Rabbit seeks security, and that is exactly what the Ox can provide. Nevertheless, this is not a balanced relationship. To the Rabbit, it can be too condescending. The refined Rabbit is indulgent and can be self-centered at times, but the hardworking Ox is enduring and unaware of the needs of the sentimental Rabbit. Meanwhile, the Rabbit will find the Ox too inflexible and pessimistic. There will be no fiery quarrels between these two, but there will be a cold war and silent resignation when things don't work out between them.

Rabbit with Tiger   6
Only if they share the same interest

The partnership between the Rabbit and the Tiger can be difficult at times, but basically, these two are both witty and understand how to get along with people. The suave Rabbit is smart enough to let the Tiger take the lead; at least, the Rabbit lets the Tiger believe this is so; in reality, the Rabbit knows just how to manipulate the Tiger to get things done. However, Tigers occasionally show their true colors by trying to dominate or bully the sensitive Rabbit. In order to make this relationship work, the couple must share some interests.

Rabbit with Rabbit   7
Why not—as long as they have loads of money

The Rabbit-Rabbit combination should work out just fine. These two share many interests and personality traits in common; they work together politely and avoid conflicts. Generally speaking, these two will try everything to maintain a peaceful and amicable relationship; after all, nobody hates confrontation more than the Rabbit. In the meantime, these two Rabbits both share their passion and love for beautiful things. They love shopping and know how to get a great bargain. Therefore, in order to maintain their high-standard lifestyle, these two will work hard together to make enough money for them to spend.

Rabbit with Dragon   5
Their differences might come between them

The Dragon loves the spotlight, and the Rabbit simply wants a peaceful and quiet life. These two share few things in common and might find each other difficult to deal with. The powerful Dragon will be the domineering one in this relationship, and the Rabbit might find the Dragon overbearing at times. As an idealist, the Dragon cannot help but demand the Rabbit to follow his or her rules. At the same time, the neat Rabbit simply cannot stand the messy and sometimes unorganized Dragon. They might find a way to compromise if they have their own space, but in the long run, their differences will become their problems.

Rabbit with Snake   6
It takes some effort to make it work

The partnership between the Rabbit and the Snake is interesting. Stability and security are what they are both looking for in a relationship. They both share a love of art and music, and all the beautiful things in life. However, they are also both calculating and selfish sometimes. When it comes to sacrifice and compromise, they always expect the other party to do the deed for them. Both are practical in nature so these two can work successfully together toward their mutual objective and goal. Although it is not the best combination, with some effort, the relationship might still stand a chance.

Rabbit with Horse   6
Why not just be friends

When these two first meet, there might be fireworks, but soon, the sparks will fade, and problems will surface. After all, the Horse enjoys action and adventure, and the Rabbit seeks tranquillity and security. On most Sundays, this couple might be arguing to stay in or go out. The active Horse enjoys outdoor activities, while the Rabbit just wants to sit back and relax in their comfortable home. The Horse's quick temper also might become too much for the peaceful Rabbit, while the Horse might find the Rabbit too passive and uninteresting. So, to make a long list of differences short, why don't you two just be friends?

Rabbit with Sheep   8
You two make a nice couple

Both searching for a peaceful and harmonious life, the Rabbit and the Sheep work perfectly together as a couple. Their shared good taste and love for beauty ensure a beautiful home and a lavish lifestyle. The Rabbit and the Sheep will have many things in common and will be both understanding and considerate with each other. The Rabbit will be the more practical among the two and is more suited to take charge of the finances. The imaginative Sheep can be the decorator of the house. Generally speaking, this partnership will be mutually beneficial and they will trust and love each other dearly.

Rabbit with Monkey   7
Amusing

These two don't have much in common. The Monkey thinks the Rabbit is dull and boring, while the Rabbit finds it hard to trust the cunning and fickle Monkey. However, these two will not confront each other head to head like the Monkey and Ox, nor will they retaliate like the Tiger and the Monkey. Instead they will open the door of communication and wait for the right time to negotiate a way to work things out. Although this relationship might work, it will be somewhat distant and tolerant.

Rabbit with Rooster   5
Maybe not

Although they are both intelligent and witty, the differences between these two might eventually come between them. The Rooster is a show-off at heart and the Rabbit simply cannot stand the Rooster's cocky attitude. The Rabbit might be turned off by the Rooster's never-ending criticism, and the Rooster will find the Rabbit indifferent and insensitive. Consequently, there will be misunderstandings and miscommunication between the two. Basically, these two don't communicate in the same channel and will often rub each other the wrong way.

Rabbit with Dog   7
As long as they don't take each other for granted

The combination of the Rabbit and the Dog will work out just fine. They will both feel comfortable enough to share their thoughts and feelings with each other, and have a basic understanding about their strengths and weaknesses. The Dog depends on the practical Rabbit to set their goals and priorities, and the Rabbit admires the Dog's loyalty and sincerity. These two types will get on well together despite their small differences. And as long as they don't take each other for granted, they can be a great team.

Rabbit with Pig   9
Very compatible—they will be happy together

The Pig is probably the best partner for the Rabbit. They are extremely compatible, and they both take time to understand each other. The Rabbit is intelligent and eager to understand the strengths and weaknesses of the Pig, while the Pig will rely on the practical Rabbit for advice and decisions. This couple knows how to appreciate the contribution of each other and also how to tolerate each other's likes and dislikes. Most of the time, the sociable Pig will be the spokesperson, and the Rabbit will be the organizer for the couple. The Rabbit and the Pig partnership will be long-lasting and fun-loving.

THE FIVE ELEMENTS:
The Rabbit—the natural element is Wood

THE METAL RABBIT: 1891, 1951, 2011

The Metal element lends the otherwise timid Rabbit some courage. This Wood-Metal combination creates Rabbits with strong confidence and absolute faith in their ability. This makes them somewhat inflexible and often disinclined to listen to advice and suggestions. After all, the Metal Rabbit is indifferent to what people think. In fact, being artistic, they have absolute faith in their taste, and art and music are the only things that can move them emotionally. People born under this sign are very artistic and visionary. They have exquisite taste in beauty and often become dedicated collectors.

THE WATER RABBIT: 1903, 1963, 2023

The Water element enhances the Rabbit's sensitive quality, so this type of Rabbit is fragile and emotional by nature. The Water Rabbit is extremely sympathetic and can relate to how others feel and so it makes sense that the Water Rabbit is usually very popular among friends. Nevertheless, Water Rabbit has the tendency to become too attached and overemotional about others' problems, which often leads him to shy away from reality. All

Rabbits hate confrontation and conflicts, particularly the sensitive Water Rabbit. They should learn to be more decisive and not to drown in self-pity.

THE WOOD RABBIT: 1915, 1975, 2035

The double-Wood element opens up the Rabbits' emotions and makes them creative and adventurous. Usually, Wood Rabbits are generous and easygoing. They want to belong and often try hard to fit in with the desired group. The Wood Rabbits' emotions and thoughts are like an open book, putting them in vulnerable spots and causing them to sometimes be taken advantage of. Wood Rabbits are patient; therefore, whatever they do, especially in a creative and artistic field, Wood Rabbits will eventually reach the top.

THE FIRE RABBIT: 1927, 1987, 2047

The Fire element helps the passionate and affectionate Rabbit open up his emotions. At the same time, Fire also makes them quick-tempered and moody. Fortunately, the Rabbits' nature will help mask their temper with charm and diplomacy. Fire Rabbit is an excellent leader, having more strength and character than any other Rabbit. In general, this type of Rabbit should learn to let reason control his or her emotion and avoid becoming too moody.

THE EARTH RABBIT: 1879, 1939, 1999

Unlike other Rabbits who avoid confrontation and conflict, Earth Rabbits are more decisive and independent and will try to overcome obstacles in their own way. Although they are materialistic and self-centered, they also know how to achieve their goals through carefully calculated moves. They are so practical compared to other types of Rabbit that they have the potential to make names for themselves through hard work.

The Celestial Dragon

Ranking order   **Fifth**

YEARS   ## ELEMENTS

1904 Feb.16	–	1905 Feb.03	Wood
1916 Feb.03	–	1917 Jan.22	Fire
1928 Jan.23	–	1929 Feb.09	Earth
1940 Feb.08	–	1941 Jan.26	Metal
1952 Jan.27	–	1953 Feb.13	Water
1964 Feb.13	–	1965 Feb.01	Wood
1976 Jan.31	–	1977 Feb.17	Fire
1988 Feb.17	–	1989 Feb.05	Earth
2000 Feb.05	–	2001 Jan.23	Metal
2012 Jan.23	–	2013 Feb.09	Water
2024 Feb.10	–	2025 Jan.28	Wood

Force:	Yang
Natural element:	Wood
Season and principal month:	Spring—April
Direction of its sign:	East 30–Southeast 30 degrees
Hours ruled by:	7A.M.–9A.M.
Best companions:	Rat, Monkey
Worst companions:	Ox, Rabbit, Dog, Dragon
Color:	Yellow

PERSONALITY CHARACTERISTICS

Positive	Negative
Compelling	Abrupt
Courageous	Arrogant
Discriminating	Defensive
Dynamic	Demanding
Energetic	Dissatisfied
Enthusiastic	Egocentric
Exciting	Emotional
Faithful	Impatient
Generous	Intolerant
Idealistic	Irritable
Intelligent	Opinionated
Irresistible	Overpowering
Lucky	Ruthless
Perfectionist	Short-tempered
Principled	Willful
Self-sufficient	
Sentimental	
Sincere	
Talented	
Visionary	

DRAGON—THE ANIMAL

The Chinese don't call themselves "the descendants of dragons" for no reason. Dragons are deeply rooted in Chinese culture and are frequently portrayed in sculptures, paintings, and temple posts. It is the only mythical animal that ever made the cut in the Chinese zodiac and, also, one of the most popular signs.

In most Chinese paintings, this magnificent creature is often portrayed as a combination of many animals—a creature with a pair of antlers like the deer, a camel head, the eyes of a hare, and the neck of a serpent. Its belly looks like that of a crocodile, and its claws like those of an eagle, its paws like tiger's and its ears like those of a buffalo. The mighty Dragon can also rise to Heaven in one second and then descend to the depths of the sea the next second.

Yet no one really knows where the Dragon comes from or has actually seen a real live Dragon. Nevertheless, for centuries, the Dragon has been a symbol of imperial power, being the celestial animal of the Chinese emperors. These emperors believed that they were the real Dragons and the sons of the Heavenly God. The Chinese refer to emperors' beds as the Dragon bed, the ceremonial dress as the Dragon robes, the throne as the Dragon seat, the palace as the Dragon palace, the heir as the Dragon child; Dragons can be seen on the buildings in the imperial palace. Dragon screens are an important part of this Dragon culture . . . the list goes on. Basically, you can put the word "Dragon" before everything owned by the emperors—everything except the "Dragon eye" (a type of fruit).

Thus, because the noble animal symbol has represented the Chinese emperors for centuries, all Chinese parents hope to have a Dragon child. It is no wonder every Dragon year has the highest birth rate in China.

DRAGON PEOPLE

Dragons are born leaders and masters of ceremonies. You are usually energetic, strong and healthy. Better yet, you are also very lucky. In fact, your good luck often helps you end up at the top of your chosen profession even though you are not especially power-hungry. And because of your magnetic, persuasive personality, you have the potential for high achievement.

Dragon people shine in the crowd. When you walk into a room, heads turn; people whisper and eyes follow your every move. You are the kind of person who grasps people's attention immediately and makes them murmur "hmmm" and wonder. But you don't get the attention by laughing loud or dressing like a clown. Sometimes it might be the mysterious scent you wear or the low, sexy voice you project. In fact, if someone meets you at a party, there's a good chance that he or she will remember you the next time you meet. Believe me, it is hard to miss a Dragon in a crowd.

Also separating you from the crowd is your excellence at competitive games. Competition thrills you, and you are often driven by your strong will to win. Nevertheless, you can also be overconfident, so you sometimes overlook the possible upset and plots that could overthrow you. And although you refuse to admit this, the truth is, Dragon people don't take failure gracefully. It's best to stay as far away from a defeated Dragon as possible. Your volcano of emotions can make the Millennium Fireworks in Paris looks like smoke from a cigarette. Luckily, a defeated Dragon is not seen often because you Dragon people usually end up as the champions. After all, you are born intelligent and fortuitous, and you are smart

enough only to fight battles you're sure you have a good chance of winning. But win or lose, you certainly know how to make the headlines.

As a Dragon, you are an idealist and a perfectionist. You are born thinking you are perfect, and this makes you quite inflexible. Honor and integrity is your middle name, and you usually set up extremely high standards and rules to live by. Furthermore, you Dragon people tend to expect those around you to follow your Himalayas-high standards—no one is allowed to question or defy your rules.

Remember the movie *Jurassic Park?* Like the powerful *T-rex* that terrorizes the park, you Dragon people are dominant and powerful. You usually walk and talk in such an assertive and confident manner that you intimidate others. Frankly, you can be very demanding and arrogant. On good days, people look up to you with awe and admiration, and on bad days, people see you as an egocentric monarch.

But the truth is that you are indeed a monarch. The leadership quality you possess is so powerful that it probably emerges during childhood. This persuasive and scrupulous personality can bring you great success or spectacular failure. To your point of view, only your way is the right way, and only your opinions are valuable. You are aggressive and determined; going after what you want is second nature to you. You are feisty and gifted with power and luck and will only settle for the best, and that is probably why you admire the rich, the famous, and the beautiful. And Dragons are definitely not the types to sit and wait; on the contrary, you usually rush out, give commands, and make things happen.

Occasionally tyrannical, you hate orders except when you are giving them. Unlike the Tiger, who imposes his will forcefully and firmly, or the Ox, whose authority is implied by his stern disposition, you know exactly how to exert authority and yet be gentle with your servants. However, Dragons are terrible snobs. Although money is not always the main object, wealth, prestige, and splendor can overly impress you.

You are born strong, healthy, and usually live a long life. But due to your hunger for power, Dragons aren't suited to growing old. The prospect of losing power, the helpless feeling of youthful strength ebbing away is unbearable to you. Irritable and stubborn, you can be a real big mouth, and many times your words often outrun your thoughts. Nevertheless, your opinions are worth listening to, and your advice is always good. So people do listen to you and your influence is considerable.

You are gifted, intelligent, tenacious, willing, and generous. Often envied by others for your good fortune and good luck, you can do anything you want. In fact, no matter whether you choose to be in art, medicine, or politics, you will shine in it. You will be a success wherever you go.

Often loved, you are never disappointed in love. In fact, you are frequently the cause of some drama or despair. Outspoken, lucky, and financially fortunate, you show boundless energy and vitality. In general, you are the healthy, sentimental visionary of the Chinese zodiac.

THE MALE DRAGON

The Male Dragon is a natural showman. He knows how to make an entrance, and he often leaves a lasting impression. He is vibrant, talented, and extremely charismatic. On the negative side, he is also arrogant, demanding, and egocentric.

Usually seductively attractive, the male Dragon is never short of admirers. He is the kind of old-fashioned man, who is conservative and sometimes can even be called a chauvinist. He is very picky in choosing his soul mate and lucky for him, his girlfriends are usually the typical James Bond movie girls—long-legged beauties who happen to hold a Harvard Ph.D. degree in nuclear engineering.

The Dragon man really believes that he will not and simply cannot make any mistake; hence, he has to be right all the time. He makes all kinds of rules, and everyone he knows must obey him. Does this description remind you of someone who was extremely authoritative to his six children and too proud to show his feelings for the governess Maria? Someone whose talented singing touched hearts and souls with the song "Edelweiss"? Doesn't he remind you of the Captain Von Trapp in the movie *The Sound of Music?* It turns out the captain really was a Dragon, and in fact, so was Maria, who was twelve years younger than the captain.

The Dragon man is positive and persuasive. Although he hates to admit it, he can be quite selfish, too. He knows exactly what he wants and how to get there, and will not allow anyone or anything to interfere with him.

He is faithful and can be sentimental and passionate toward his loved ones. Unpredictable and impulsive at times, he is an adventurer at heart, but not a daredevil. Always vibrant and enthusiastic, success comes to him easily. He is the happiest when he feels respected and desired and loves to give advice. He wants people to realize he is irreplaceable. Never a graceful loser, a Dragon man can be overconfident. He always sets his goal high, too high sometimes, but he will listen to no one and truly believes he can achieve anything.

Despite being associated with health and vitality, his ambition and busy mind can sometimes cause him insomnia and respiratory problems. Fortunately, the male Dragon rarely gets very sick, and if he ever does, he normally recovers quickly.

In relationships, the Dragon can be egocentric and aristocratic. A traditionalist, he is the gentleman who will open doors or pull up chairs for a lady. He can be romantic when in private and is very generous with loved ones. Never short of any admirers, the Dragon man often marries young or remains single throughout his life.

THE FEMALE DRAGON

Physically attractive, the female Dragon is hard to resist. Usually she grew up being the center of attention and will exude self-confidence and charisma wherever she goes. In fact, Dragon and Tiger ladies are the two most attractive women in the Chinese zodiac.

She sees the world in black and white and believes strongly in her judgment. She is honest and frank and does not hesitate to speak her mind, even when the topic is controversial. She is a doer and can't stand injustice. Most likely she will be the one to collect thousands of signatures on a petition for a good cause she truly believes in.

Being so talented and energetic, she always ends up in the winner's circle, and whatever she does, she puts out 120 percent effort and throws her heart and soul into the game. Go check out your Dragon woman friend's house—she probably has trophies stacked up in her living room—trophies from bridge to golf tournaments. She is not used to defeat, nor will she accept it. In fact, a Dragon woman only recognizes two kinds of people—the winners and the losers. Passionate believers for equal rights, Dragon women insist that what a man can do, she can do better. But it's always important for men and women to remember never to underestimate a Dragon lady.

Financially, the female Dragon is quite generous to her family and friends, and, of course, herself. She never cares too much about her bank balance and is the type of person who will pick up anything she likes in the store without even bothering to check the price tag. Ask her the price of the diamond earrings she wears, she will mostly likely tell you she signed the bill without even checking the figure. Therefore, it is wise not to put her in charge of your finances.

Family and friends are important to her, and she will never turn down a friend in need or in trouble. Chances are, she will give you whatever you need and help you out any way she can, but meanwhile, brace yourself for a long imperial speech from this Dragon woman preaching her morality and standards.

In relationships, she will not be happy being a housewife. She constantly needs to set new goals to keep her busy. As a born perfectionist, she demands attention and insists on applying her high standards to her loved ones. Finally, there is nothing she hates more than deception and manipulation; therefore, remember never to cross a Dragon woman because her grudge is lasting and her revenge will be disastrous.

DRAGON AT WORK

Dragons are not power-hungry people; however, with their luck and intelligence, they always end up at the top of their chosen professions. Usually noticed when young, Dragons set their goals at a tender age.

Dragons suffer from mild claustrophobia, so they need a lot of space and freedom. Therefore, it is unlikely to find a Dragon working in a small room on tedious and mundane tasks. They need to work in an open environment, where they can work independently and utilize their talents and intelligence.

As a boss, Dragons feel right at home in a position to give orders and directions. And their skills and demands are legendary; they are definitely not the types of bosses who sit around and do nothing. Instead, they might be in Amsterdam for a business meeting one day, and in Taipei the next day. Sometimes, one cannot help but wonder where Dragons get all this energy.

As a partner, Dragons can be arrogant and difficult. After all, for persons who believe they are always right, there is no room for negotiation or compromise. In fact, most Dragons prefer to work alone rather than have a partner, and if they ever do, the partner must be someone the Dragons can completely trust and rely on. Their counterpart must be business-oriented, never leaving the finances to the generous Dragon, and must find a way to calm the overpowering Dragon.

As a colleague, the Dragon is irresistible and noble-hearted. They will never turn down a coworker in need. Most of the time, they do this not because they are so compassionate, but because they see this as their duty. However, this idealistic individual is a perfectionist and expects colleagues to hold the same standards in their daily behavior. The Dragon is usually someone who likes to hang out with coworkers but has absolutely no patience with those who are not punctual.

Generally speaking, with their authoritative attitude and charisma, Dragon people will do well as lawyers, CEOs, or film directors. John Lennon and Dr. Martin Luther King, Jr. are just two famous Dragon people.

BEST DRAGON OCCUPATIONS

Advertising executive	Performer
Architect	Philosopher
Artist	Photojournalist
Astronaut	President or
Chairman	prime minister
Doctor	Professional speaker
Film producer	Salesperson
Film star	War correspondent
Lawyer	

FAMOUS DRAGONS

Bruce Lee	Robin Williams
Charles Darwin	Roseanne Barr
John Lennon	Salvador Dali
Kirk Douglas	Shirley Temple
Martin Luther King, Jr.	Tom Jones
Ringo Starr	

COMPATIBILITY

The Chinese believe each animal sign is most compatible with signs that are four years apart, and least compatible with the sign that is six years apart. Based on this concept, a circle can be drawn with all signs, locating the Triangle of Affinity and the Circle of Conflict.

TRIANGLE OF AFFINITY
Dragon, Monkey, Rat are the Triangle of Affinity

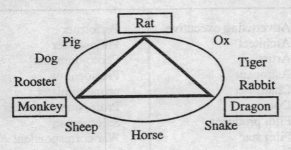

CIRCLE OF CONFLICT
Dragon's conflict sign is Dog

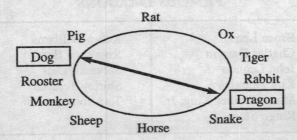

Signs	Rating 1–10	Relationship
Dragon with Rat	9	One of the best-arranged unions
Dragon with Ox	5	Don't, the two of you will fight constantly
Dragon with Tiger	7	Despite minor difficulties, it's good for marriage
Dragon with Rabbit	5	Their differences might come between them
Dragon with Dragon	5	They'll always compete against each other
Dragon with Snake	7	This might work
Dragon with Horse	7	Love at first sight but might go downhill
Dragon with Sheep	7	A sound and stable relationship
Dragon with Monkey	8	This could work—they admire each other
Dragon with Rooster	8	You two make a good couple together
Dragon with Dog	*4*	*Really you can do better than that*
Dragon with Pig	7	Balanced but not passionate

Dragon with Rat   *9*
One of the best-arranged unions

The Dragon and the Rat's relationship is probably the best of all combinations. The Chinese believe this is the best match for both marriage and partnerships. The Rat will welcome the Dragon's dominance and the Dragon will admire the Rat's intelligence. Both are powerful and aggressive, and can work hand in hand to make things happen. With their mutual self-confidence and talent, neither will be threatened by the other and will in fact admire and support the other to bring out the best in them. Whatever they do, as long as they do it together, these two will achieve success, happiness, and prosperity. This is an absolutely marvelous combination.

Dragon with Ox   5
Don't, the two of you will fight constantly

When the powerful and dominant Dragon is put together with the inflexible and stubborn Ox, the result is a constantly fighting combo. Being the practical one in the relationship, the Ox likes to stick by the rules and follows daily routines. On the contrary, the willful Dragon does not like to play by the rules and is idealistic and unpractical about the future and reality. They often fight over dominance, and each believes only their own way is the right way. They do have strong physical attraction but the relationship might not be long-lived.

Dragon with Tiger   7
Despite minor difficulties it's good for marriage

A relationship between the passionate and powerful Tiger and Dragon will never be boring. Both are highly motivated, and action-oriented—quite a match. They are equally talented and demanding, and they aren't intimidated by each other. The Dragon provides a strong influence on the Tiger; however, the Tiger has better business sense. Similar in temperament, they actually understand each other better than most people predict, and since they are both frank and straightforward, they won't avoid talking about their problems.

Dragon with Rabbit 5
Their differences might come between them

The Dragon loves the spotlight, and the Rabbit simply wants a peaceful and quiet life. These two share little in common and might find each other difficult to deal with. The powerful Dragon will be the domineering one in this relationship, and the Rabbit might find the Dragon overbearing. As an idealist, the Dragon often can't help but demand the Rabbit to follow his or her rules. At the same time, the neat Rabbit simply can't stand the messy and sometimes unorganized Dragon. They might find a way to compromise if they have their own space, but in the long run, their differences will become their problems.

Dragon with Dragon 5
They'll always compete against each other

In any Chinese paintings of two Dragons, a close look will reveal that these two Dragons are always fighting for something. This definitely hints at what the Dragon-Dragon combination will be like. In fact, since these two Dragons share the same personality traits, they will share the same desire to fight for leadership and dominate. Both inflexible and demanding, neither will back off and surrender. The Dragons know what they want in life and will not compromise in any circumstances. In the end, these two will be competing against each other constantly.

Dragon with Snake   7
This might work

In some Chinese folklore, Snakes are considered small Dragons. Therefore, this partnership between the Dragon and the small Dragon should work just fine. In this relationship, the Snake is the schemer and the Dragon executes the plan. Being the spokesperson of the two, the Dragon is outgoing and aggressive, and the intelligent Snake often works quietly behind the scenes to plan for the future. These two are equally bright and ambitious, but the Snake's secretive nature might make it hard for the Dragon to understand and communicate at times. In order for this union to work, the Dragon has to be less dominant and the Snake needs to be more open.

Dragon with Horse   7
Love at first sight but might go downhill

Both the Dragon and the Horse are emotional, so when they first meet, it could be love at first sight, nothing but fireworks and sparks. Nevertheless, it usually starts going downhill from there. This doesn't mean this relationship does not stand a chance; actually, these two get along all right, but the relationship just isn't as intense and passionate as when it started. The Dragon and the Horse are both aggressive and impatient, so they often lose their tempers fast, but fortunately, they also know how to communicate and speak up about their disagreements or grudges. Eventually, if they learn to respect and pay more attention to each other, the relationship will work.

Dragon with Sheep   7
A sound and stable relationship

Without a doubt, when the Dragon and the Sheep join together, the Dragon will be the dominant partner in the relationship. Indeed, the passive Sheep will welcome the Dragon's leadership wholeheartedly. The Sheep will be attracted to the vibrant and energetic Dragon, and the Dragon will appreciate the creativity and sensitivity in the Sheep. Although sometimes, Sheep might have problems voicing their frustration, they also hate confrontation and will try to avoid it. In general, this will be a sound and stable relationship, but these two should learn how to bring the best out of each other and keep their communication channel clear.

Dragon with Monkey   8
This could work—they admire each other

The union of the Monkey and the Dragon is one of the best among all combinations. Both powerful and intelligent, they communicate at the same level and share the same vision and interest in many things. Both have great instinct, and know exactly how to handle and please the other. Overall, whether in love or in business relations, Monkey and Dragon can make a successful team.

Dragon with Rooster   8
You two make a good couple

The combination of the Dragon and Rooster can be a fine one. The Dragon admires the Rooster's talents and intelligence, while the Rooster appreciates the Dragon's confidence and stamina. Both are optimistic and sometimes a little cocky, but they will work well together toward a mutual goal, and with their talents and wits, they will succeed eventually. Meanwhile, these two types both enjoy being in the spotlight, so there might be a time when these two are fighting over it. Nevertheless, they both know not to let their argument get out of hand, so in general these two will make a good couple together.

Dragon with Dog   4
Really you can do better than that

This relationship is definitely not recommended. The Dragon is full of grand plans, and although not all of them are feasible, the cautious Dog won't hesitate to criticize the Dragon and deflate the Dragon's big ego. At the same time, the Dragon cannot stand the cynical Dog and dislikes every dream and vision being questioned. There is a serious communication problem between these two. The partner will misinterpret most of the things said, and it isn't a pretty picture when a fuming Dragon argues with a barking Dog. It might be smarter to stay away from each other.

Dragon with Pig   7
Balanced but not passionate

Although the Dragon and the Pig do not share much in common, these two will have a balanced relationship. They probably are not as passionate as some of the other combinations, but at least they will respect and admire each other. The Pig adores the confident Dragon and welcomes the Dragon's leadership, while the Dragon appreciates the honest and easygoing nature of the Pig. Of course, the Dragon can be a little egotistical when you compare him or her with the Pig's big charitable heart. But they will be compatible and enjoy each other's company. This will be a long-lasting relationship.

THE FIVE ELEMENTS:
The Dragon—the natural element is Wood

THE METAL DRAGON: 1880, 1940, 2000

The Metal element strengthens the Dragons' many qualities. Metal Dragons are usually extremely bright and expressive. They have great vision and are burning with determination and ambition, but at the same time they are also unbending and unwilling to accept defeat. Metal Dragons could be the most strong-willed of the Dragons. They usually succeed because they will most likely burn the bridges behind them and leave nowhere to turn but to go on. That is the kind of personality the Metal Dragons possess.

On the negative side, Metal Dragons have very little patience with others, especially those who are considered inferior, and can be extremely intense and critical to others. They have high standards and morality, and it is useless to try to convince them of beliefs other than their own.

THE WATER DRAGON: 1892, 1952, 2012

The Water element brings calmness and balance to the Dragons' personality. This makes them less selfish and more open to suggestions or criticisms. Unlike the other Dragons, the Water Dragons tend to be more diplomatic and will not judge others or jump to any conclusions too quickly before further observation. They are wise, reliable, and creative, and excellent negotiators.

On the negative side, Water Dragons can be overoptimistic and unrealistic. This optimism may sometimes prevent them from seeing clearly. They should learn to recognize what is feasible and what is not, and try to make the right choice.

THE WOOD DRAGON: 1904, 1964, 2024

Wood represents growth and renewal; therefore, this double-Wood element brings stability to the Wood Dragon. The Wood Dragon is probably the most creative and innovative among all Dragons. They enjoy exploring new things and don't care so much about their ego as other Dragons. They are very good at analysis and theory and are guided by logic and reason. Generous and cooperative, the Wood Dragon can work with others and always tries to avoid offending anyone. Nevertheless, when challenged, the Wood Dragon will be fearless and powerful like most Dragons.

THE FIRE DRAGON: 1916, 1976, 2036

The combination of Fire and Wood creates the most competitive and outgoing of all Dragons—the Fire Dragon. As a perfectionist, the Fire Dragon can be extremely critical of others and impatient with faults and foolishness. These Fire Dragons are full of charisma, which is probably why many of the Fire Dragons end up being famous. Holding a high standard in everything, the Fire Dragon expects a lot from everyone. This type of Dragon is short-tempered, so better remember that it's not safe to cross one unless you'd like to burn in his or her outburst of flames. Nevertheless, the Fire Dragons are born leaders and carry a sense of superiority and authority within their very presence. If they can learn to be more sensitive and considerate, they can become great leaders.

THE EARTH DRAGON: 1868, 1928, 1988

The Earth element helps the natural Wood element to grow, and thus brings patience, stability, and security to the Earth Dragon. This type of Dragon is usually more cooperative and sociable than other Dragons, and doesn't pay as much attention to details. Unlike Fire Dragons or Metal Dragons, Earth Dragons are not in such a hurry, tend to be fair, and avoid jumping to any conclusions before they understand the entire situation. They don't lose their tempers easily, but once they do, you'd be safer if you were miles away from them.

The Diplomatic Snake

Ranking order	Sixth

YEARS				ELEMENTS
1905 Feb.04	–	1906 Jan.24		Wood
1917 Jan.23	–	1918 Feb.10		Fire
1929 Feb.10	–	1930 Jan.29		Earth
1941 Jan.27	–	1942 Feb.14		Metal
1953 Feb.14	–	1954 Feb.02		Water
1965 Feb.02	–	1966 Jan.20		Wood
1977 Feb.18	–	1978 Feb.06		Fire
1989 Feb.06	–	1990 Jan.26		Earth
2001 Jan.24	–	2002 Feb.11		Metal
2013 Feb.10	–	2014 Jan.30		Water
2025 Jan.29	–	2026 Feb.16		Wood

Force:	Yin
Natural element:	Fire
Season and principal month:	Spring—May
Direction of its sign:	South 30–Southeast 60 degrees
Hours ruled by:	9A.M.–11A.M.
Best companions:	Ox, Rooster
Worst companions:	Tiger, Monkey, Pig
Color:	Green, Red

PERSONALITY CHARACTERISTICS

Positive	Negative
Amusing	Anxious
Charitable	Calculating
Clever	Cruel
Compassionate	Dishonest
Curious	Indifferent
Determined	Intense
Discreet	Jealous
Elegant	Judgmental
Fun-loving	Mean with money
Gregarious	Pessimistic
Honorable	Possessive
Organized	Remote
Perceptive	Self-doubting
Profound	Self-righteous
Reflective	Suspicious
Self-contained	
Sensual	
Sympathetic	
Well mannered	
Wise	

SNAKE—THE ANIMAL

Both in Western and Eastern cultures snakes have always been the seducers of human beings. In the Bible, the Snake was the one who tempted Eve to taste the "forbidden fruit" and is perceived as a symbol of sin and evil. But in Chinese culture, Snakes are considered wise and good-hearted. In fact, just as caterpillars will transform into butterflies, Snakes are considered to be the form Dragons take before their transformation.

There is a famous Chinese folk story about a Lady White Snake, who matured over centuries, gaining her power and magic until, eventually, she takes the form of a human being. Lady White Snake learned all kinds of magic and tricks through masters and the Buddha and used her power to help the needy. She transformed into a woman just so that she could help a young man who once saved her life (as a Snake) many years before.

She married the young man and lived happily for years until one Dragon boat festival. Not knowing that Lady White Snake was actually a spirit, the husband brought back a pot of realgar wine, which is believed to drive away evil spirits. After taking a sip, Lady White Snake could no longer hold her human form and, in-evitably, appeared as a huge white snake in front of her husband. Astonished and frightened, the poor man was shocked to death. When she came to and resumed her human form, Lady White Snake was heartbroken to find her husband dead. She then began a long and difficult search to obtain a celestial herb that could save her husband's life.

"Lady White Snake" is a fascinating story about love and deceit, gratitude and sacrifice. It also reveals the ro-mantic and human side to the Snake's character.

SNAKE PEOPLE

Born under the sign of wisdom, you are intelligent and wise, naturally charming and popular. You are very attractive and can lure people like a magnet. Although it is hard to describe, the Snake definitely has that certain something that makes you so alluring and sexy. Different from the Snake who seduced Eve into sin, the Snake in Chinese astrology is not evil or dark, but is, in fact, a sexy, normal human being.

Unlike the Rat and the Monkey, who tend to talk without taking a breath, you prefer to be the observer in any situation. Quiet and reserved, communication and negotiation are not your strong suit; instead, you are quite good at giving advice. It is no surprise that most of your friends rely on you for advice and direction, and you seldom disappoint them.

However, you prefer to give advice than to receive it. Furthermore, you will never ask anyone for advice. You are not a social butterfly like the Pig or the Monkey, and you also hide your emotions well. Some think you are egocentric, and many times they are right. You refuse to listen to others and do not judge based on facts or reasons—how can they be right? You know yourself too well, and you have such a strong belief in yourself that you trust only your own intuition and judgment.

You are a deep thinker who is always looking for opportunities. You like to meditate and plan. And, you are very mysterious because you don't reveal your emotions or your thoughts to anyone. You have such a strong distrust for others that you are very secretive. And your memory is so good that if anyone crosses you, you can hold the grudge for years without ever expressing any feelings. Then one day, when the time is right and it is least expected, boom, you strike back without any mercy.

You are a spotlight magnet, and you won't be ignored. Peer group attention and public recognition are the least of what you expect. Yet you are never noisy or deliberately outspoken, and you have an excellent manner.

Some people associate the Snake with laziness because Snakes like to lie still under the desert sun. In fact, Snakes are hardworking people who are determined and talented. A deep thinker and highly intelligent, you plan before you move and you know instinctively how to do things in the most efficient way. You can get the job done in the quickest and most economical way, while everyone else is only half-finished. This is probably why you have the time and luxury to relax afterward.

You make your decisions quickly and firmly. And your confidence can be your best friend or your worst enemy. When things do not go your way, the failure will crush your ego. You will refuse to accept the defeat and see the whole thing as unfair. Determined to follow through with anything you undertake to the bitter end, you detest being left up in the air.

Elegant and sensual, you treat yourself well and enjoy the good things in life, such as good books, food, music, and theater. You can be quite philosophical sometimes; you'd rather rely on your gut feeling than someone else's advice. Amazingly, you are right most of the time, causing people to think you have a sixth sense or are a little psychic.

Many of the century's most beautiful women and powerful men were born in the year of Snake, people like Jacqueline Onassis, John F. Kennedy, Abraham Lincoln, and Grace Kelly. It is no wonder that most people at some point of their lives are secretly or hopelessly in love with a Snake. Snake people are slightly dangerous and charmingly smart as well as diplomatic, polite, and romantic.

Paradoxically you are an intellectual philosopher, a cerebral person yet you rely heavily on first impressions, your gut feelings, on your sympathies, rather than on facts, or the advice and opinions of others. You choose your friends carefully and can be extremely generous to them with your time and advice. But, you also insist on the same loyalty from your friends. And when it comes to lending money, you can be a bit cheap. Though your sympathy for others often leads you to offer help, the fatal flaw in your character is your tendency to exaggerate—about helping friends as with everything else. If you do somebody a favor, you sometimes become possessive toward them in an odd way.

Another flaw in your character is that though you never "waste time in idle gossip, you are capable of lying." White lies, true lies, whatever you call them, though you don't lie often, you do lie when you feel you can absolutely get away with it.

Financially, you will have good luck. Actually you don't have to worry, as you'll always be able to lay your hands on money when it's needed. Generally speaking, Snakes are fiscally careful but generous with friends and family. You should stick to careers that won't involve any risk—even the risk of working too hard.

In love, Snake men are romantic, charming and have a sense of humor while the Snake women are usually beautiful and successful. But when you choose a partner, you will be jealous and possessive—even if you no longer love the person. Rejection is the worst blow to your delicate ego. The Snake must be received, welcomed, accepted, and approved by those with whom they come in contact. You need a lot of security.

THE MALE SNAKE

Most male Snakes are powerful. That power, combined with their charm and intelligence, allows them to succeed in almost any field they dedicate themselves to. The Snake is usually very influential on the people around him, and he is very aware of it. Attractive and irresistible, the Snake man knows just how to use his charm wisely to get what he wants.

Not only is he usually very handsome, romantic, and passionate, but his sense of humor is unbeatable, which is why so many women cannot help but fall for him. Nevertheless, this Don Juan wanna-be can be very flirtatious, so for those of you who are involved with a Snake man, you'd better watch him closely. After all, fidelity to him is just an eight-letter word that is not in his dictionary. But things will improve after he is tamed and settled down; the Snake man will be a great father when he is committed to being one.

The Snake man is very confident and knows how to show off his intelligence or charm subtly. He knows that some of his old guy friends think he is a snob. To him, image is everything, and he will try anything to maintain a certain image of his.

Snake man does not know how to cope with failure. He is one lousy loser. He cannot tolerate insults and truly believes in "an eye for an eye." He is a deep thinker but always keeps his thoughts private. Always observing, waiting, and calculating, he is one creature you do not want to cross because a Snake never forgives or forgets.

If anyone damages his image or reputation, Snake man will keep a memo in mind and will find the best time to strike back for revenge.

The majority of Snake men are financially successful and lucky with money. The male Snake usually has a great sense of business and can be quite successful in negotiation. He trusts his gut feelings and intuition over facts or logic.

This outward confidence masks the Snake man's insecurity. Especially when it comes to the people he loves, this anxiety can manifest into jealousy and possessiveness, which can sometimes push them away instead.

THE FEMALE SNAKE

The lady Snake is always attractive. She often glides through the room with a cool demeanor and certain grace. Her style and beauty are undeniable and her taste in fashion is often admired. It is not a surprise that many men are instantly captivated by her after once glance. And just like the Medusa who lured young men to her cave and turned them into stone, the lady Snake can turn any young man into a lovesick puppy.

Although guys line up just to have a dance with her at a party, lady Snake chooses her partner carefully. For her, only the best will do. He must be attractive, polite, and intelligent. Once she locks her eyes on someone, she will not let anyone or anything stand in her way.

Lady Snake is witty and humorous and quite popular among her female friends as well. She is amiable and sensual and always shows her compassion and sympathy. As a shrewd thinker, she gives great advice and knows just how to help you get out of a sticky situation.

Luckily, even with her image as a seducer, the female

Snake is more faithful than the male Snake. She can be flirtatious occasionally, but she knows not to cross the line and get into trouble. Nevertheless, Snake woman is known for her jealousy and possessiveness. Even if there is no affection left anymore, she will see the partner as her property.

Born with a sixth sense, the Snake lady is keen and observant. Her mysterious psychic feelings are usually right on target. Determined and thoughtful, she does not waste time on the useless chitchat and always goes straight to her point. Once she sets her goal, nothing can stop her from going after it.

Snake lady is uncannily perceptive. She takes failure personally and will always remember how others treat her. If someone did her a big favor, she will make a note of it and find the right time to show her appreciation. On the other hand, if someone rubs her the wrong way, you can be sure that she will wait and calculate, and finally retaliate with a vengeance.

SNAKE AT WORK

Snakes are efficient people. They are clever and capable and do not like to waste time. They like to plan and calculate everything ahead, and then proceed in the most cost- and time-effective way.

They can be counted on to carry a project through to its end, although Snakes are not known for having long projects. They can make decisions quickly and firmly, and once they've made up their minds, Snakes will fight hard for anything they believe and allow nothing to stand in their way.

Calculating and mysterious, Snakes know exactly how to eliminate the competition quietly. They are very confident and rely heavily on their intuition. Logic and facts do not mean much to them because the only thing they believe in is themselves.

As a boss, the Snake has certain expectations of their staffs. Disliking changes and insecurity, the Snakes will train the staff well in hopes of keeping them for years. And because of their suspicious nature, Snakes will only depend on a very few key people and usually trust no one to run the company for them.

As a partner, the Snake is cautious and suspicious. They do not form partnerships easily, and when they decide to do so, they will surely be doing tons of investigation before they sign that little piece of paper. But the good news is once they commit to the partnership, they will be extremely devoted and make sure to see that the project succeeds till the end.

As a colleague, the Snake is considerate and sensitive. They do not like to pry into coworkers' lives and often work successfully in a team environment. Snakes are good counselors, but they don't offer their advice voluntarily; instead, they like to be quiet and observant, collecting information that they exchange with no one. Always looking out for an opportunity, the Snakes know how to showcase their talents for the right promotion or get themselves noticed.

Generally speaking, with their great intelligence and diplomatic skills, Snakes will do well in politics. Franklin D. Roosevelt, Mao Tse-Tung, and John F. Kennedy are just three famous Snake people.

BEST SNAKE OCCUPATIONS

Ambassador
Astrologer
Clairvoyant
Diviner
Fortune-teller
Interior designer
Linguist
Mediator
Personnel officer

Politician
Professor
Psychiatrist
Psychologist
Public relations
  executive
Restaurant owner
Teacher

FAMOUS SNAKES

Abraham Lincoln
Alfred Nobel
Audrey Hepburn
Brooke Shields
Franklin D. Roosevelt
Grace Kelly
Henri Matisse
Howard Stern

Jacqueline Kennedy
Onassis
John F. Kennedy
Mao Tse-Tung
Mohandas K. Gandhi
Oprah Winfrey
Pablo Picasso

COMPATIBILITY

The Chinese believe each animal sign is most compatible
with signs that are four years apart, and least compatible
with the sign that is six years apart. Based on this

concept, a circle can be drawn with all signs, locating the Triangle of Affinity and the Circle of Conflict.

TRIANGLE OF AFFINITY
Snake, Rooster, Ox are the Triangle of Affinity

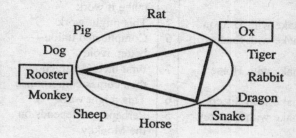

CIRCLE OF CONFLICT
Snake's conflict sign is Pig

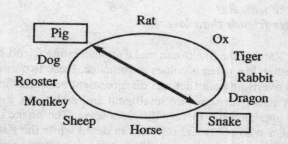

Signs	Rating 1–10	Relationship
Snake with Rat	6	Better friends than lovers
Snake with Ox	8	This union can be a good one
Snake with Tiger	4	Difficult to know what they see in each other
Snake with Rabbit	6	It takes some effort to make it work
Snake with Dragon	7	This might work
Snake with Snake	6	Complicated union—better avoid
Snake with Horse	7	First there's attraction then comes compromise
Snake with Sheep	6	This might work
Snake with Monkey	5	Perhaps—it depends on the Monkey
Snake with Rooster	9	A love connection omens favorable
Snake with Dog	7	A balanced and compatible team
Snake with Pig	4	*The Pig can never please the Snake*

Snake with Rat   *6*
Better friends than lovers

The Rat and the Snake can make an interesting friendship together, but when it comes to romance, these two might find overriding conflict and disagreement between them. Although both signs are intelligent and ambitious, these two approach life in very different ways. The Snake is a thinker who plans and schemes in detail while the Rat is actually an aggressive doer. They can be attracted to each other at the beginning, but as the infatuation fades, the Snake will pull away from the Rat and keep secrets.

Snake with Ox   8
This union can be a good one

Finally, the Ox finds an equal partner in this Ox-Snake relationship. This will make a lasting partnership because they know how to respect and share with each other. The dependent Ox will give the ambitious Snake all the support he or she needs. The Snake will have a stronger influence over the Ox than the other way around, but the Ox will not mind a bit because the Ox enjoys feeling needed by the Snake. Both are practical planners, they enjoy working toward long-term goals.

Snake with Tiger   4
Difficult to know what they see in each other

The combination of the Tiger and the Snake will be a difficult one; after all, these two don't share much in common and they approach life from very different angles and perspectives. The dramatic Tiger is more outspoken than the Snake and likes to follow gut feelings instead of the head. On the contrary, the secretive Snake is always suspicious of everyone, including the Tiger, and prefers to organize things in a more systematic way. There will be conflicts between the two owing to some misunderstanding.

Snake with Rabbit   6
It takes some effort to make it work

The partnership between the Rabbit and the Snake is interesting. Stability and security are what they are both looking for in a relationship. They both share a love of art and music, and all the beautiful things in life, but at the same time, they are also both calculating and selfish sometimes. When it comes to sacrifice and compromise, they always expect the other party to do the deed for them. Both are practical in nature, these two can work successfully together toward their mutual objective and goal. Although it is not the best combination, with some effort, the relationship might still stand a chance.

Snake with Dragon   7
This might work

In some Chinese folktales, Snakes are considered small Dragons. Therefore, this partnership between the Dragon and the small Dragon should work just fine. The Snake is the schemer in this relationship and the Dragon executes the plan. Being the spokesperson of the two, the Dragon is outgoing and aggressive, and the intelligent Snake often works quietly behind the scene to plan for the future. These two are equally bright and ambitious, but the Snake's secretive nature can make it hard for Dragon to understand and communicate at times. In order for this relationship to survive, the Dragon has to be less dominant and the Snake needs to be more communicative.

Snake with Snake   6
Complicated union—better avoid

The two Snakes combination can be tricky. While sharing the same personal traits, the same weaknesses and strengths, these two appear to understand each other. They are both patient, enduring, and ambitious; they don't jump and attack their prey like a Tiger. Instead, they wait and observe until the prey comes to them voluntarily. So, these two Snakes will work fine together as business partners focused on the same goal. Nevertheless, the secretive Snake is always suspicious of the other and tends to hide important thoughts from the other. Neither likes to be dominated; yet one Snake might smother the other. And their jealous natures can sometimes get out of hand. Perhaps it is better to avoid this partnership.

Snake with Horse   7
First there's attraction then comes compromise

When these two first meet, there will be strong attraction between them. But as the sparks fade, the combination of the Snake and the Horse seems to be less exciting. In fact, the Snake and the Horse are two very different types who think and act in almost the opposite directions. The Snake is passive and cautious, while the Horse is active and daring. Gradually, the Horse will find the passive Snake boring, and the Snake will think the fickle Horse annoying. Unless they both share the same goal and learn to appreciate each other and compromise, the relationship is bound for some bumps.

Snake with Sheep   6
This might work

The scheming Snake is the thinker who plans carefully, and the sensitive Sheep is the artist who is creative. They both share a love for the arts and the fine things in life and will get along well because neither of them is comfortable with confrontation. Yet the Snake is often the one in charge of the two, while the Sheep enjoys being laid-back and is more than happy to let the Snake take over. Nevertheless, they can probably benefit through this union. Still, the Snake may get tired of the Sheep's sentimental nature, and the Sheep will feel insecure from the Snake's secretive personality.

Snake with Monkey   **5**
Perhaps—it depends on the Monkey

At the beginning, these two find the other mysterious and intriguing, but pretty soon, the attraction will wear off, and they will start finding faults in each other. The Snake can't tolerate the show-off Monkey who can be mischievous and cunning sometimes, and the Monkey will tire of the enigmatic Snake people, who tend to keep their thoughts to themselves. "Talk to me!" the Monkey will say. Communication will become a problem, and the relationship might be rocky.

Snake with Rooster   **9**
A love connection omens favorable

This is another love connection recommended by the Chinese. The Snake and the Rooster understand and admire each other for their talents and ability. Both of them are ambitious and focused workaholics. The Snake will be the schemer who plans carefully, and the Rooster will be the executor who carries out the scheme. Intelligent and capable, this team is bound to succeed to their mutual benefit when they put their heads together. This will be a loving and balanced relationship.

Snake with Dog   *7*
A balanced and compatible team

The Snake and the Dog will get along fine together. The Dog admires the Snake's intelligence and talents while the Dog's loyalty and dedication touch the Snake. This will be a balanced and compatible relationship. Both are idealistic and have a good understanding of each other's weaknesses and strengths. The Dog is smart to overlook the Snake's secretive and selfish nature, and in return, the Snake learns to accept the Dog's nagging. If they have similar goals to work toward together, they are most likely to succeed.

Snake with Pig   *4*
The Pig can never please the Snake

Being conflicted opposite signs in the Chinese zodiac, the Snake and the Pig tend to see only each other's faults. The Pig will be annoyed by the Snake's secretive and jealous personality, and the Snake will find the Pig naïve and careless. After all, the cautious Snake always observes and plans everything in detail, and the fact that the Pig often just dives into any relationship without reservation can be disturbing to the Snake. Although forgiving and enduring, the Pig will find it a mission impossible to please the Snake.

THE FIVE ELEMENTS:
The Snake—the natural element is Fire

THE METAL SNAKE: 1881, 1941, 2001

The Metal element strengthens the Snake. Snake people are usually proud and confident and Metal Snakes know exactly what they want in their lives; they are hungry for luxury and wealth, and usually possess the extreme willpower needed to get what they want. This type of Snake is very calculating, possessive, and domineering. They are always looking for opportunity and planning schemes that can help them achieve their goal. The Metal Snakes like to plan alone; they are very secretive because they don't trust others easily. Yet, despite their intelligence, they don't guarantee to achieve their goals, but beware, Metal Snake definitely won't accept failure gracefully.

THE WATER SNAKE: 1893, 1953, 2013

When you combine the calm and intuitive Water element with the secretive and intelligent Snake, you get a strong manager with much to offer. Water Snakes are very business-minded and full of charisma; they know exactly how to manage people and projects and are extremely focused. They are wise and insightful, yet practical and artistic. They don't get distracted away from their goals and always have their ways to influence those around them. But remember, a Snake is always a Snake; never cross one of these Water Snakes because their excellent memories enable them to bear grudges a long time. Someday, they might turn around and bite you on the neck.

THE WOOD SNAKE: 1905, 1965, 2025

The Wood Snake is one of the exceptions. They are wise, but not as ambitious, knowledgeable, but not as selfish. These types of people are usually more laid-back and easygoing; they love to work in a creative or innovative environment without too much restriction or too many rules to tie them down. Nevertheless, like most Snake people, Wood Snakes still crave the life of luxury and care about their own appearance. It is no wonder that many Wood Snake people are poets, painters, musicians, or collectors.

THE FIRE SNAKE: 1857, 1917, 1977

The Fire element, added to the Snakes' natural Fire element, makes the Fire Snakes dynamic people. Many Fire Snakes end up as politicians because they are full of charisma and energy and show extreme confidence and leadership, which make people run to vote for them. Intensive and passionate, Fire Snakes express their extreme emotion to both their lovers and their enemies. Like most Snakes, the Fire Snake is suspicious and insecure by nature and doesn't trust people readily. Nevertheless, their hunger for power and fame and their intelligence and ambition always take them to the top.

THE EARTH SNAKE: 1869, 1929, 1989

The Earth element brings calmness and stability to the Snake. This makes the Earth Snake less mysterious and ambitious, more like the rest of the Snakes. Yet slowly and patiently, they still reach the goal, just not in as grand a scale. The Earth Snake is usually warm and easygoing, reliable, and communicative. Being the most graceful and enchanting of all Snakes, the Earth Snake tries not to be suspicious and can be loyal and honest to friends and family. They usually have great sense of money; they know about what to invest in and when to stop. The Earth Snake sees the best in people and tries to avoid conflict.

The Productive Horse

Ranking order   Seventh

YEARS

				ELEMENTS
1906 Jan.25	–	1907 Feb.12		Fire
1918 Feb.11	–	1919 Jan.31		Earth
1930 Jan.30	–	1931 Jan.16		Metal
1942 Feb.15	–	1943 Feb.04		Water
1954 Feb.03	–	1955 Jan.23		Wood
1966 Jan.21	–	1967 Feb.08		Fire
1978 Feb.07	–	1979 Jan.27		Earth
1990 Jan.27	–	1991 Feb.14		Metal
2002 Feb.12	–	2003 Jan.31		Water
2014 Jan.31	–	2015 Feb.18		Wood
2026 Feb.17	–	2027 Feb.05		Fire

Force:	Yang
Natural element:	Fire
Season and principal month:	Summer—June
Direction of its sign:	Direct South +30 and -30 degrees
Hours ruled by:	11 A.M.–1 P.M.
Best companions:	Tiger, Dog
Worst companions:	Rat, Ox, Rabbit, Horse
Color:	Orange

PERSONALITY CHARACTERISTICS

Positive	Negative
Agreeable	Anxious
Amusing	Careless
Calm	Contradictory
Charming	Disobedient
Cheerful	Hard-nosed
Confident	Hot-tempered
Curious	Impatient
Energetic	Insecure
Enterprising	Irresponsible
Enthusiastic	Moody
Flexible	Opportunistic
Generous	Self-serving
Independent	Show-offy
Logical	Superficial
Loyal	Unstable
Persuasive	
Popular	
Sincere	
Sociable	
Talented	

HORSE—THE ANIMAL

Within minutes of birth, horses will struggle to stand up and eventually start walking in no time. It is no wonder people born in the year of the Horse are considered strong, agile free spirits.

In China, Horses are the symbol of freedom and are often associated with grace, bravery, and individuality. As one of the major animals used for transportation in ancient China, horses represent speed and perception. In fact, many Chinese idioms are associated with this noble creature such as the one about someone who is "like a horse that grows only in the number of teeth and nothing else." Thus implying this person has accomplished nothing despite their advanced age; this is usually a polite and modest way to talk about yourself. Another Chinese expression used to wish someone good luck and success is "Maa-Dauh-Cherng-Gung"; thus implying immediate success, just like the arrival of a running horse.

According to the Chinese zodiac, and in Japan, the most controversial element combination is probably the Fire Horse. The addition of powerful and voracious fire to the uncontrollably independent nature of the Horse makes for an ambitious and extremely headstrong Fire Horse.

In conservative ancient societies like China or Japan, where individuality was not encouraged and rebelliousness was forbidden, Fire Horse people were not popular among friends and family. Correspondingly, the Fire Horse year usually had the lowest birth rate compared with other years. Fortunately, in today's society, it isn't considered wrong to be independent, ambitious, and individualistic. So, the true colors of the Fire Horse can finally be truly appreciated.

HORSE PEOPLE

Born under the sign of ardor, Horse people are active and energetic. You are quite confident and eager to try new things. To you, life is like a voyage, and you simply can't wait to discover what is ahead of you. Independent and versatile, you can do everything on your own, you listen to no one and refuse any offers of help. Enthusiastic and frank, you are quite lovable and easy to get along with.

You care a great deal about how others perceive you. You've got plenty of sex appeal and know how to dress to impress instead of to show off your style or fashion. Clothes in bright colors are your top choices, and you enjoy admiring yourself in front of the mirror. You like to exercise outdoors, and you're usually wearing a tan. You make sure you always look your best.

Charming and cheerful, you are very likable. Your vivacity and enthusiasm make you popular. Most of the time, you hang out with a regular group of friends. Nevertheless, unlike Rabbits, who like to stay at their own "level," Horse people have friends from all walks of life. On Monday, you might have dinner with a friend who works at the White House, and then on Thursday you will be out drinking with your butcher friend.

You love being in a crowd and are quite a party animal. Normally, some people will feel uncomfortable if they are left alone in a party where they don't know anyone. But not you, the curious and sociable Horse. Meeting new friends makes your heart run wild, and the larger the party, the more strangers, the better. Perhaps this is why you can usually be seen at such events as concerts, plays, meetings, and sporting events. Comfortable in a crowd and talkative, you are indeed quite a persuasive speaker. Talented and convincing, you are the kind of person who is not afraid to speak up. And you are too honorable and candid to back down when facing unfairness.

It follows, then, that you are the kind of person who will stop when you see a car accident. After calling for help, you will probably listen to both sides of the story, then start making your own comments and conclusions. Before anyone notices, you will actually be lecturing to a small crowd about road safety and the law. Impulsive as you appear, you know how to sway your audience and when it is the right time to stop for applause—thus demonstrating your forthrightness and talent as a natural public speaker.

You are very keen and observant, and you always seem one step ahead of anyone else and can finish their thoughts before they have a chance to finish them. Nevertheless, in truth you recognize that you are really more cunning than intelligent. That is probably why you desire to project a confident exterior, but underneath, you feel somewhat insecure and unconfident.

You are very hardheaded and stubborn. Capable of instant mood swings and fiery temper, you can be very difficult to deal with sometimes. You resent any pressure or controls and hate to be cornered, instead preferring to do things your own way. And when someone rubs you the wrong way, you do not wait patiently for the right moment to retaliate like the Snake; instead, you bite and kick and fight back without hesitation. Then often, you find yourself feeling remorse and regret for your quick temper and harsh words.

The Chinese believe that the Horse is born to race and travel; therefore, all Horses invariably leave home at a young age. Accordingly, you are the adventurous type and are fascinated by foreign cultures and lifestyles. Traveling is your number one hobby and you are always planning for your next trip. Freedom and independence are as important to you as air and water. Free-spirited and lively, you do not stay in one place for long; you need plenty of room to roam, and you cannot stand schedules, timetables, petty rules, and regulations. You simply don't have the patience or time.

Being born in the year of the Horse, you have many contradictory aspects in your character. You are proud yet sweet-natured, confident yet insecure, arrogant yet modest, productive yet impatient, and, in love relationships, jealous but tolerant. You need your independence but always long to belong to a group; you love to talk and persuade people but refuse to listen to others. You crave intimacy but are afraid to be cornered and dependent. The truth is, no matter how integrated you seem to be, you still remain powerfully rebellious in your heart. And although you have boundless energy and ambition, nevertheless, you have a hard time belonging.

In matters of money and the heart, you seem hot-blooded, hotheaded, and impatient, you are quite an egoist. To say it as bluntly as a Horse would, you are simply quite selfish sometimes. It is very rare to see a Horse listening to others' problems and offering advice, in reality; you are interested in problems only if they are your own. You are quite skilled at handling money and make a good financier. Unfortunately, you are also known for suddenly losing interest in something. When it comes to love, you can suddenly become weak and uncertain. A romantic at heart, you will give up everything just for love. But in love and money, you are so rebellious and impatient that you change your mind constantly and often lose interest in a project even before it is completed.

Most of the time you are cheerful, passionate and romantic. A gifted sweet talker, you know how to capture a lady's heart. Free-spirited and open-minded, no secret is safe with you because you always blurt it out accidentally. You are sporty and smart, and you enjoy physical and mental exercise. Creative and fun, adventurous and innovative; you are always ready to try new things. Challenges excite you, and it follows that routines simply bore you.

THE MALE HORSE

The male Horse has many attractive qualities. He is ambitious and creative, independent and energetic, humorous and passionate, and definitely a partygoer. Although he doesn't usually stand out from the crowd at the first glance, as soon as he starts talking, people will be impressed by his persuasive speech and fascinated by his agile mind.

The male Horse doesn't have the patience to manage his own finances, and can be considered as a spendthrift sometimes. Impulsive and superficial, he craves approval from others and sometimes spends too much time on how he looks. A skilled communicator and a productive character, he has very low tolerance for people who are unenthusiastic, uninterested, and uncommunicative.

The male Horse often has a good memory; he is especially good at jokes and stories. He can remember perfectly a funny joke or story he overheard somewhere and then recite it to friends with thrilling narration and vivid description. A vibrant character, he always talks with rapid but graceful body movements and animated facial expressions. In most cases, he will usually respond quickly to interesting discussions and creative ideas. This ability to make snap decisions is another illustration of his agile mind.

Horses, both male and female, usually leave home young. For the male Horse, even while only a boy, he would have dreamed of traveling to exotic places, exploring new lands, or discovering a new planet. He is a dreamer and loves new ideas. As soon as a new idea surfaces, he simply will get involved at full speed without bothering to evaluate the feasibility. Uninterested in any kind of routines or timetables, he detests all kinds of bureaucracy and prefers to be his own master. He is easily bored and does not take criticism too well. Insecure and unsteady as he appears, however, a stable home is quite important to the Horse. Unsurprisingly, therefore, the more often he travels, the more he will appreciate his sweet home.

Although he wants a stable home, he can't really be described as a family man. If you are in love with a male Horse, understand that his need for space is like water and air to you. Give him the freedom he longs for, and, eventually, he will return home—although he'll hardly ever offer to help with the housework. He is honest, noble, and sociable and appears to be cheerful and easygoing. Nevertheless, he should learn to control his bursting temperament and be less egocentric. He is not the hide-and-seek type who wants you to guess what he really implies underneath his comments; in fact, he is naturally straightforward and often offends others without even realizing it.

In general, the Horse man must learn to think with his head instead his heart, be less impulsive and indecisive, and, eventually, he'll become his own master and find the peace in his heart.

THE FEMALE HORSE

The female Horse is usually elegant and well groomed. Quick-witted and mentally alert, she is also independent and industrious. Always cheerful and humorous, she enjoys making people laugh and is quite popular. She is never the shy wallflower who sits quietly in the corner, waiting for her Prince Charming to rescue her. Nor is she the prom queen who draws curious eyes wherever she goes; instead, she is just one energetic and sociable individual who will approach any new face in a party and start making friends and conversation.

And like many women, the female Horse craves flattery and attention. But an overconfident female Horse can't stand being ignored, and she will sometimes go too far to get the attention of a particular individual she has her eye on. Normally, she is not a knockout like Sharon Stone; nevertheless, she is sensual and very sexy in her own way.

The female Horse has many likable qualities. Clever but not necessarily intelligent, she is talented in public relations. Good at promoting events and ideas, she is a persuasive speaker who knows how to use this skill for her own benefit. But she's not the manipulative type who gets you to do things for her without you even knowing that you're being used. Straightforward and frank, this Horse woman doesn't beat around the bush.

Her mind is naturally inclined to business, and she enjoys beginning new projects. Her desire to be involved in all kinds of work makes staying at home doing nothing totally unacceptable. Resourceful and productive, she enjoys working, but definitely doesn't excel in nine-to-five bureaucratic jobs. She doesn't respond well to authority and won't tolerate a subordinate role. Three famous women, Barbra Streisand, Cindy Crawford, and Janet Jackson are Horses who keep their hands full of different projects. Inactivity bores the female Horse to death.

A horse is born to run and to explore. So the Horse woman usually leaves home at a tender age to go on a voyage to exotic places. Born with a free spirit and stubborn personality, she does not listen to anyone and usually turns away from any criticism or complaint. Some may think she appears selfish at times, because she simply has neither the time nor patience for the problems of others. Also on her list of dislikes are schedules and timetables; in fact, she has a poor sense of timing. Her friends always expect the female Horse to be behind schedule. This chronic lateness could be the result of admiring herself in front of the mirror too long, or it could be simply her way to rebel against any possible control or restraint on her freedom.

Hot-blooded and hotheaded, she likes dramatic scenes and movies, and is actually quite capable of creating them, too. Her impulsive mood swings can be disastrous. However, though she is proud and rebellious, she is actually quite a softy when it comes to love. When she falls in love, she loses all sense and logic. Nevertheless, it is still possible for her to soon get tired of the person, and eventually she'll move on to search for the next object of her affection.

In general, this female Horse is smart and sexy. She needs to bring out her talents more and has potential for success in business and public relations. However, she must learn to be more sensitive to others' needs and more patient and less impulsive.

HORSE AT WORK

Energetic and enterprising Horses are usually very devoted to their jobs, especially when they don't feel trapped and forced to work. Bureaucrats bore them, and schedules mean nothing to them. In fact, any job that follows routines and timetables will not be suitable for the free-spirited and independent Horses. They need jobs with variety to entice and challenge their versatile nature.

Typical doers, Horses have a low threshold for boredom, though they can turn into autonomous and productive working machines if they find something interests them. Determined and strong-minded, once they set their goals, they will go after them with full force. Famous for their impatience, Horses talk fast, think fast, and eat a lot faster than average people. Somehow, they have a tendency to ignore details and cannot be trusted with delicate works and secrets. Creative and logical, they are better at initiating a new project rather than actually carrying it through to completion. After all, they are easily panicked, moody, and unorganized; sometimes they tend to drop a project halfway through simply because they lose interest in the project.

As a boss, the Horse is popular. Since they detest authority, they don't like to be authoritative. So, they are not the kinds of bosses who stand behind you and supervise your every move. Rather, the Horse boss believes everyone should know his or her own responsibilities and duties and not need to be reminded all the time. Nevertheless, occasionally, the Horses' impulsive and impatient side will kick in, and when that happens, those who work for them might suffer from the sudden change of mind and will be forced to shift to a completely new project without even finishing the previous one.

As a partner, Horses have gifted business minds and are always keen on new projects and ideas. Their enthusiasm can easily persuade others to invest in these projects. However, easily panicked, they can be irresponsible when they are in a moody moment. Horses need a supportive and understanding counterpart to calm them down.

As a colleague, the Horse is energetic and fun to be with. Gregarious and charming, the Horse can always be found in a group. Feeling that they belong to a group is very important to them, although Horses can be loners at times—they crave to be accepted. Open-minded and adventurous, they are always the first one to volunteer for new things. Coworkers should be aware of the Horses' talkative nature; their secrets will not be safe with the chatty Horse.

Generally, with their superb communication skills and productive minds, the Horse will do well in PR, and showbiz. Clint Eastwood, Harrison Ford, and John Travolta are other famous Horse people.

BEST HORSE OCCUPATIONS

Administrator	Hairdresser
Advertising executive	Inventor
Architect	Painter
Artist	Poet
Athlete	Politician
Chauffeur	Reporter
Chemist	Salesman
Cowboy	Soldier
Doctor	Teacher
Entertainer	Technician
	Tour guide

FAMOUS HORSES

Antonio Vivaldi
Barbra Streisand
Cindy Crawford
Clint Eastwood
Frederic Chopin
Harrison Ford
Igor Stravinsky
Ingmar Bergman
Isaac Newton
Janet Jackson

John Travolta
Kevin Costner
Leonard Bernstein
Mike Tyson
Paul McCartney
Sandra Bullock
Sean Connery
Theodore Roosevelt
Thomas Edison

COMPATIBILITY

The Chinese believe each animal sign is most compatible with signs that are four years apart, and least compatible with the sign that is six years apart. Based on this concept, a circle can be drawn with all signs, locating the Triangle of Affinity and the Circle of Conflict.

TRIANGLE OF AFFINITY
Tiger, Horse, and Dog are the Triangle of Affinity

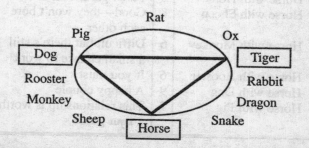

CIRCLE OF CONFLICT

Horse's conflict sign is Rat

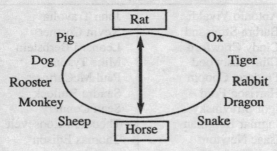

Signs	Rating 1–10	Relationship
Horse with Rat	**3**	***No no no—run away now***
Horse with Ox	5	Unfortunately they will part
Horse with Tiger	8	Why not—they have lots in common
Horse with Rabbit	6	Why not just be friends
Horse with Dragon	7	Love at first sight but might go downhill
Horse with Snake	7	First there's attraction then comes compromise
Horse with Horse	6	Better partners than lovers
Horse with Sheep	8	Good—they won't bore each other
Horse with Monkey	6	Difficult but there's still a small chance to work
Horse with Rooster	6	If you must
Horse with Dog	9	A happy couple
Horse with Pig	7	This relationship is worth a try

Horse with Rat   3
No no no—run away now

Being six years apart from the Horse, the Rat is the conflicted opposite of the Horse. It goes without saying that these two are not only incompatible, but they'd better stay away from each other. The self-centered Horse can't understand the kind, sentimental Rat. Although they thought opposites attract, the fact is, they see things in a totally different perspective, and, eventually, the Rat will be craving security but the impatient and moody Horse just can't settle down. Till the end, the Rat is most likely to be mistreated and suffer in this relationship.

Horse with Ox   5
Unfortunately they will part

The Ox and the Horse move at different paces and often think in different directions. The conventional Ox is cautious and likes to play by the rules, whereas the wild Horse prefers to be impulsive and risky. This irresponsible and adventurous nature of the Horse can really drive the patient Ox crazy, and eventually the Ox will walk away from the relationship. Both are lousy at communication, and both are anxious to lead. When things don't go the way they want, each tends to blame the other.

Horse with Tiger   8
Why not—they have lots in common

Finally, here is a couple that shares much in common and enjoys each other's company. Both Tiger and Horse are impulsive and are definitely not the types to wait. In fact, usually they are so impatient that they jump right into things they are passionate about. Although they sometimes still argue like any couple, at least they know each other so well that their quarrels usually don't last too long. Better yet, the patient Horse knows how to tame and comfort a Tiger in depression. Both parties will benefit from this partnership.

Horse with Rabbit   6
Why not just be friends

When these two first meet, there might be fireworks, but soon, the sparks will fade, and problems will surface. After all, the Horse craves action and adventure, and the Rabbit seeks tranquillity and security. On most Sundays, this couple might be arguing about staying in or going out. The active Horse enjoys outdoor activities, while the Rabbit just wants to sit back and relax in the comfort of home. The Horse's quick temper also might become too much for the peaceful Rabbit, while the Horse might find the Rabbit too passive and uninteresting. So, to make a long list of differences short, why don't you two just be friends?

Horse with Dragon   7
Love at first sight but might go downhill

Both the Dragon and the Horse are emotional, so when they first meet, it could be love at first sight; they'll see nothing but fireworks and sparks in their eyes. Nevertheless, it usually starts going downhill from there. This doesn't mean this relationship does not stand a chance; in fact, these two get along just fine, but the relationship just isn't as intense and passionate as when it started. The Dragon and the Horse are both aggressive and impatient, so they often lose their tempers too fast. Fortunately, they also know how to communicate and resolve their disagreement or grudge. Eventually, if they learn to respect and pay more attention to the other, the relationship will work.

Horse with Snake   7
First there's attraction, then comes compromise

When these two first meet, there's a strong attraction between them. But as the sparks fade, the combination of the Snake and the Horse seems to be less exciting. In fact, the Snake and the Horse are two very different types who think and act almost in opposite directions. The Snake is passive and cautious, while the Horse is active and daring. Gradually, the Horse will find the passive Snake boring, and the Snake will become annoyed by the fickle Horse. Unless they both share the same goal, and learn to appreciate each other and compromise, the relationship is bound to have some rocky bumps.

Horse with Horse   6
Better partners than lovers

The double-Horse combination creates two Horses running at the same speed toward the same goals. This combination works well as a business partnership because they are equally restless and determined. On the other hand, they also change their minds a lot, so the project or the business usually takes longer than expected to complete. When in a romantic relationship, these two

Horses will struggle with their egos and might argue over which direction they should be heading. Impatient at heart, the Horses will find it difficult to settle down with each other.

Horse with Sheep   8
Good—they won't bore each other

This combination of the Horse and the Sheep will always be exciting. The Horse gives the insecure Sheep confidence and direction and can help the Sheep manage its creative talents and business. Both dislike sticking to any routine, so this couple will live by their own rules. They are both indecisive and, therefore, change their mind constantly. While this trait often annoys people in other animal signs, the Horse and the Sheep understand and tolerate each other. This will be quite an interesting couple who won't bore each other.

Horse with Monkey   6
Difficult but there's still a small chance it will work

The Horse and the Monkey will get along fine with each other most of the time. Because they are both flexible and accepting, they won't be struggling for dominance and can cooperate and solve any conflicts that occur. However, the Monkey may feel insecure around the impatient and restless Horse. And the Horse's inability to open up will bring tension between these two and cause communication problems. If these two can find their own rhythm and learn to work things out, there might still be a chance of success in their union.

Horse with Rooster   6
If you must

The witty Horse and the smart Rooster are equal in their intelligence and talents. At the beginning, these two complement each other's strengths. Nevertheless, as time goes by, the impatient Horse might find the Rooster too critical and demanding. Moreover, the Rooster simply can't understand why the Horse wants to spread itself so thin on too many projects and can't seem to remain devoted to or focused on one thing. Once the Rooster shows his or her argumentative nature, the quick-tempered Horse will be annoyed and ready to walk away.

Horse with Dog   9
A happy couple

Finally, this is a good example of how opposites attract. The Horse and the Dog don't appear to share anything in common, but their differences actually complement each other just fine. The Horse is independent and aggressive, and the Dog is generous and sensitive. The loyal Dog will not mind the Horse's dominance and will follow the Horse on their travels. The Horse appreciates the Dog's communicative and considerate nature and finds it easy to share thoughts and ideas with the Dog. Neither of them is competitive and will enjoy each other's company while maintaining their own independence. They make a happy couple.

Horse with Pig   7
This relationship is worth a try

The Horse and the Pig seem to get along just fine. The popular and sociable Pig enjoys parties and so does the fun-loving Horse. The Horse enjoys the Pig's generous and affectionate nature, while the Pig finds the Horse's independence attractive. However, both the Horse and the Pig are stubborn and cannot be rubbed the wrong way. At some point, the mischievous Horse may try to test the limits of the Pig's tolerance. In order to succeed, the couple needs to communicate better and compromise for each other.

THE FIVE ELEMENTS:
The Horse—the natural element is Fire

THE METAL HORSE: 1870, 1930, 1990

The Metal element makes this type of Horse more stubborn than other types of Horses. Usually headstrong and irrepressible, the Metal Horse can be very self-centered and will listen to no one. The Metal Horse can be very productive when motivated and is constantly looking for new excitement and challenges, but he needs a lot of stimulation and freedom to stop him from being bored to death. This type of person dislikes supervision and can be extremely irresponsible.

THE WATER HORSE: 1882, 1942, 2002

The Water element adds more creativity to the Horse. They appreciate the arts and all the beautiful things in life, and also like to choose colorful clothes. They can cheerfully adjust to any changes in their environment. The combination of elusive water and the easily distracted Horse creates people with very short attention spans. Water Horses have the habit of changing their minds in an instant to a completely new direction without giving any reason, and this inconsistency in personality can be extremely annoying if they happen to be the boss. The Water Horse should learn to be more considerate for others and avoid constantly changing plans.

THE WOOD HORSE: 1894, 1954, 2014

Unlike the usually nervous Horse people, the Wood Horse is friendly and cheerful, calm and cooperative, and always tries to help others. Meanwhile, this makes them more gullible, and they should learn to protect themselves from being taken advantage of. The Wood Horse also has an open mind and enjoys trying new ideas instead of doing things the old-fashioned way. Though the Horses' nature makes them strong, high-spirited, and always on the run, the Wood element helps them keep their minds clear, and they become more communicative.

THE FIRE HORSE: 1906, 1966, 2026

The double-Fire element multiplies all the good and bad in Horse's qualities. In ancient times, the Chinese considered people born under the sign of Fire Horse as either advantageous or disastrous. Some women even tried to avoid giving birth during the year of Fire Horse. But the truth is that Fire Horses are exceptional people and are usually extremely passionate and easily excited. This is a person with super intelligence and energy. Although resistant to authority, they are hot-blooded and guided by great ideas. The Fire Horse may choose to have several professions and travel all over the world. The Fire Horse is constantly seeking thrills and adventures, and is capable of great success or dismal failure.

THE EARTH HORSE: 1918, 1978, 2038

The Earth element can calm the busy Horse down a little bit. Unlike the other types of Horses, the Earth Horse doesn't object so much to authority and is less flighty in general. They move slower than others and are cautious about every step. And because of their capricious nature about details, Earth Horses can be good investors or project managers who see things through from beginning to the end. Nevertheless, this cautious nature also makes them hesitant; they like to observe and consider every possibility before making a decision.

The Gentle Sheep

Ranking order	Eighth

YEARS | ELEMENTS

1907 Feb.13	–	1908 Feb.01		Fire
1919 Feb.01	–	1920 Feb.19		Earth
1931 Feb.17	–	1932 Feb.05		Metal
1943 Feb.05	–	1944 Jan.24		Water
1955 Jan.24	–	1956 Feb.11		Wood
1967 Feb.09	–	1968 Jan.29		Fire
1979 Jan.28	–	1980 Feb.15		Earth
1991 Feb.15	–	1992 Feb.03		Metal
2003 Feb.01	–	2004 Jan.21		Water
2015 Feb.10	–	2016 Feb.07		Wood
2027 Feb.06	–	2028 Jan.25		Fire

Force:	Yin
Natural element:	Fire
Season and principal month:	Summer—July
Direction of its sign:	Southwest 30 degrees
Hours ruled by:	1P.M.–3P.M.
Best companions:	Rabbit, Pig
Worst companions:	Rat, Ox, Dog
Color:	Sky-blue

PERSONALITY CHARACTERISTICS

Positive	Negative
Adaptable	Anxious
Appealing	Careless
Candid	Disorganized
Cheerful	Illogical
Compliant	Impractical
Creative	Impulsive
Easygoing	Indecisive
Elegant	Indulgent
Empathetic	Irrational
Faithful	Irresponsible
Generous	Lazy
Gentle	Pessimistic
Honest	Self-pitying
Imaginative	Unsatisfied
Independent	Vengeful
Peaceful	
Polite	
Romantic	
Sensitive	
Sincere	

SHEEP—THE ANIMAL

Generally speaking, Sheep are gentle animals. Their milk and meat are considered great nourishment. A flock of sheep lives by the "follow the leader" rule. This social pattern is demonstrated by the strong bond between mother and offspring; the young follow their mother, who continues to follow her mother. And as the pattern continues, every sheep in the flock eventually follows the oldest female sheep, who is also the leader. It is no wonder people who are born in the year of the Sheep are seen as obedient and somewhat feminine.

In China, Sheep are less important than hogs and cattle; however, they do figure in many Chinese idioms. Idioms such as "Wool comes from the Sheep's back" imply that whatever benefits someone receives, someone has to pay for, and the idiom "Sheep in Tiger's skin" indicates someone who is outwardly impressive but lacking in substance inside.

One of the well-known facts about Sheep is that they drink their mother's milk with their knees down, which is the common way in ancient China to show respect to parents, teachers, and VIPs. Thus, Chinese see these animals as the symbol of filial piety.

Sheep are also considered to be an auspicious animal. Even its Chinese character is derived from the character of the word which means auspicious.

SHEEP PEOPLE

Born under the sign of art, you are sensitive and talented. You are extremely creative, elegant, and charming. Peace-loving, ardent, and easygoing, you can get along with nearly everyone. People born under this sign are viewed as the most artistic and feminine sign of the Chinese zodiac. You are also very delicate; in fact, your good manners and charm always bring many admirers and friends.

When in a crowd, you do not stand out like the Dragon or the Tiger, as people born under the sign of Dragon and Tiger have a magnetic presence that can immediately draw attention. But for Sheep people, you are really more of an acquired taste; you don't want all the attention anyway, preferring to enjoy your peaceful, quiet moments. However, as soon as your talents in art or music are discovered, everyone will be amazed and mesmerized by you and wonder how could they have missed this magnificent person in the first place.

You are extremely sensitive and compassionate, which explains why you are easily moved by any story you hear and will sob at a Disney movie. Easygoing and peaceful, you want to make everyone happy and will avoid conflict and confrontation. It's no wonder you hardly make any enemies, as there is nothing you hate more than argument.

Although appearing calm and serene, underneath the tranquil surface you are actually very insecure. You need to feel admired and protected, and have a constant craving for love. You must have heard this too many times from your friends and family, but listen up gentle Sheep: You must learn to relax a little bit! You seem to worry too much, and it is truly unnecessary to have all this anxiety over inconsequential things.

Some call you a pessimist and you do have the tendency to shy away from major responsibilities. But this makes you quite a good team player. Your reserved nature compels you to pull back when faced with heavy decision-making. Always seeking guidance, you would much rather have others make the call and be the one to shout out "Let's go," then you will be glad to follow the leader and play by the rules.

Sheep people are dreamers. Sometimes, you are hesitant and overanxious worriers, and, worst of all, you can be remarkably indecisive. You are the type who will agonize for days before buying a pair of shoes, or will consult a dozen friends before buying a new hat. And although you don't like to admit this, you can be lazy sometimes. You lack real ambition; indeed, you would definitely choose to marry a wealthy person so you can sit back, relax, and enjoy the easy life.

Your surroundings are very important to you. Your home will be filled with stylish furniture and original paintings and sculptures due to your extraordinary taste in art and culture, and you often prefer to live in the country so you can be close to nature. Although beautiful, your home will be untidy. After all, the artist in you thinks it is too much work to clean up the house. Besides, you find it is easier to find things when they are all lying around.

Business is definitely not the strength in the seemingly disorganized Sheep. Instead, you will make a good craftsman or artist or writer and can confidently take up any career demanding artistic talents and creativity.

Sheep people are often religious and like to study the esoteric to learn more about the unknown. The mysterious and the supernatural fascinate you. But don't worry, you aren't the type of fanatic who will leave everything behind and join a cult. That is just too extreme for the peace-loving Sheep, who only wants an easy life. So, you will stop practicing your religious interest when it starts interfering with your comfort and daily routine. Still, you are a faithful reader who follows the daily horoscope in the newspaper or even a frequent caller to the 1-800 psychic hot-line to find out more about your future. And sometimes, you might decide to study the topic in detail and become a fortune-teller yourself.

Also, you are quite obsessed with your appearance, and this plays an enormous part in your sense of personal stability. Your artistic sense makes you attracted to the beautiful things in life, and you want to ensure you always look your best as you have a certain reputation to maintain. You are the type of person who will dress up nicely and put on some makeup even if you are only going to open the door to pick up your Sunday paper.

You are quite emotional and experience mood swings occasionally. If lacking the security and stability you crave, you tend to become depressed and dispirited. You need a lot of love, attention, and reassurance. In matters of love, your heart often rules your head. You are very romantic, sensitive, sweet, and darling though in a relationship, you can sometimes be a too bossy and lazy. And if the romance is going quite well, you will not hesitate to tell your partner what you want. However, there will be no power struggle because you are usually more than happy to let your partner be in charge. And it is hard to resist the gentle and caring Sheep.

THE MALE SHEEP

In general, the male Sheep is imaginative and creative. He is very easygoing and friendly, and makes few enemies. Born under the sign of art, Sheep man has a highly developed aesthetic sense. He loves beautiful things in life and has a keen eye for design and art. Although seemingly shy and reserved, he is assured when it comes to his artistic and creative sense. He is quite often sought after to give suggestions on decoration and interior design, and his opinions are usually highly regarded and respected.

Gentle and kind, he sometimes seems a little too sensitive for a man. Easily hurt and offended, this male Sheep takes comments and criticism very personally. Sometimes it is kind of exhausting for his friends because they always have to watch what they say for fear that Mr. Sheep might take it the wrong way. And when this happens, it usually takes a lot of comfort and reassurance to assure him that it was meant otherwise.

The male Sheep is very sweet; he is the type who takes notes and remembers the birthdays and anniversaries of loved ones. For one who is in love with a Mr. Sheep, prepare yourself for a lot of surprises and gifts, as he is quite generous with the one he loves. He also has a natural flair for hospitality and thus can make an exceptional host when he throws a party. He is not a flashy host, but he certainly knows how to make his guests feel at home. And he has many friends to invite.

Friends and family play an important part in his life. He enjoys good relationships with his family members and is quite dependent on them—even after he starts his own family. He is quite good with children and animals and can make a fun and creative parent. Though sometimes appearing irresponsible, this male Sheep wants to have fun but without responsibility. He shies away from major decisions and prefers his partner to take the initiative.

He is quite a softy, though definitely not a pushover. Easily moved by his emotions for others, the Sheep man can be moody. And, although people say that real men don't cry, if you look closely you will discover moisture around his eyes after watching a touching story. But don't worry about him; in reality, women find his sensitive nature attractive and irresistible.

Overall, the male Sheep is one refined and intelligent man who has a keen eye for beauty. He is a great husband who is sensitive and romantic, although tending to be chauvinistic at times. He does not like conflict and strict schedules and prefers to live a stable and comforting life. If he can get rid of his fretful and indecisive nature and concentrate on his talents, he can be quite successful in life.

THE FEMALE SHEEP

Feminine and elegant, Sheep lady is gentle, kindhearted, and sensual. She is often beautiful, slender, and lovely, too. Though definitely not the flashy type who will immediately grab your attention, she is usually quiet among the crowd and often appears to be shy—a lady of few words. Nevertheless, once you get to know her better, she will feel more at ease and will open to you.

Propriety and a beautiful environment are quite important to the gentle and peaceful Sheep woman. She desires a peaceful spot of her own so she can escape any disturbance and pressure. Her house is often very nice because Sheep have a keen eye for art and culture. However, the female Sheep can be a little untidy. She just doesn't like to clean it up herself; she tends to save this job for her maid or her family.

The female Sheep is a great friend. She is extremely dedicated to her friends and will do anything to help her friends out. But at the same time, she is quite a lucky star herself; whenever she needs a helping hand, someone or something will turn up to save her day.

Capable of mood swings, the female sheep is probably

the most emotional of all signs; nevertheless, she always keeps her composure in front of the crowd and only reveals her inner turbulence to those she trusts. She can be determined if she chooses to be, but most of the time the Sheep woman has a strong desire to depend on someone. So anyone who is dating a Sheep lady needs to be prepared for her moody moments and give her all the attention you can possibly give. This female Sheep is one who demands constant attention and reassurance of your love for her. Female Sheep can be good wives who prefer not to argue, although they won't do much housework and often need recognition from their husbands.

Impressionable and easily led, the female Sheep's naturally interested in the mysterious and the unknown. Often a faithful follower of astrology, be it Western, Chinese, or Indian, this curious soul will devour anything and listen only to what she wants to hear.

The female Sheep is usually very talented. She is the kind of person who will be awarded as the "all-around" honor student at the graduation. Never hostile or hysterical, she loves to lead a carefree existence. Candid and honest, she despises any injustice, but unlike the dauntless Tiger, who will jump out and roar at the unfairness, Sheep lady will surrender to her peaceful nature and choose to keep quiet.

In general, the Sheep woman is a gentle soul who fears rejection and criticism. She needs security to blossom and is constantly in search of someone whom she can depend on. Although she is quite sought after and often surrounded by suitors, she should still learn to control her mood swings and become more independent and confident.

SHEEP AT WORK

In reality, if Sheep have any choice, they will no doubt choose to marry a wealthy millionaire and never work again. Although talented and smart, Sheep are born free-spirited, and the artists in them detest any routines and pressure.

Sheep are inspired by the arts and love anything concerned with harmony and beauty. This appreciation often seems like laziness, as the Sheep is one laid-back creature, not especially active or hardworking. For them, a job is a job, it is not something they are willing to devote twenty-two hours a day to, or even give up their sleep for. The exception to this is when they are extremely fascinated by the work. Just like van Gogh, who worked fanatically just to finish an inspiration in his head, Sheep will become obsessive if they are totally involved in their work and projects. And if they do have some money, Sheep will be better off seeking advice on how to invest it wisely rather than using it to start their own business.

As a boss, Sheep often seek guidance because they are not sure of themselves. They often manage with an easy-going style. After all, they hate conflict and pressure, and will avoid inflicting it on their staff. If you work for a Sheep boss, you must learn to accept their constant changes in decisions.

As a partner, Sheep rely heavily on their partners. Disliking responsibility and decisions, the Sheep will leave all the major work to the partner. However, the Sheep is born with intelligence and an eye for detail and can be a great help especially if the business is in Fashion or Art. Overall, Sheep need a strong and confident counterpart to give them constant support and encouragement.

As a colleague, the Sheep is wonderful to hang out

with and is quite popular. Trustworthy and caring, Sheep often take good care of their friends and can be very generous with them. In return, Sheep will expect lots of attention and often are quite dependent once they feel comfortable in confiding in someone.

Due to their sensitive nature and their keen sense of beauty, Sheep are most suited to occupations that seek new and creative ideas and avoid routines and schedules.

BEST SHEEP OCCUPATIONS

Actor/actress	Novelist
Astrologer	Painter
Dancer	Poet
Entertainer	Potter
Fortune-teller	Story writer
Investor	Television presenter
Landscape gardener	Vocalist
Musician	Weaver

FAMOUS SHEEP

Barbara Walters	Julia Roberts
Bill Gates	Lord Byron
Bruce Willis	Mark Twain
Coco Chanel	Mel Gibson
Harry Connick Jr.	Michelangelo
Jane Austen	Robert De Niro
John Denver	

COMPATIBILITY

The Chinese believe each animal sign ... ...bout with signs that are four years apar... ... ... with the sign that is six years apa... ...ce with this a circle can be drawn with all... of Affinity and the Circle ...

... the Sheep the ... to say, these two ... punctual and stubborn ... of time. The Ox is disci- ... icial to the sloppy and disor- ... ntually, the Ox will get tired of ... ss left by the Sheep all the time and ... Although some may say opposites at- trac... just don't see eye to eye.

Sheep with Tiger   2
One of the worst combinations

There is a famous Chinese saying about sending a Sheep directly to a Tiger, which implies a situation that is doomed or suicidal. After all, as soon as the Tiger sees the Sheep, he will not hesitate to attack and devour this poor animal. This is probably why most Chinese believe the Tiger-Sheep combination is one of the worst combina- tions. The soft and indecisive Sheep will be controlled and manipulated by the bossy Tiger. And the gentle nature of the Sheep will probably drive the impatient and im- pulsive Tiger crazy. If these two form a family, the somewhat lazy Sheep will refuse to do the dishes and the aggressive Tiger will also not pick up the housework. These two just don't want to compromise.

Sheep with Rabbit   8
You two make a nice couple

As both are searching for a peaceful and harmonious life, the Sheep and the Rabbit work perfectly together as a couple. Their mutual good taste and love for beauty ensure a beautiful home and a lavish lifestyle. The Rabbit and the Sheep will find many things in common and will be understanding and considerate with each other. The Rabbit will be the more practical and is more suited to take charge of the finances, while the imaginative Sheep can decorate the house. Generally speaking, this partnership will be beneficial to both and they will trust and love each other dearly.

Sheep with Dragon   7
A sound and stable relationship

Without a doubt, when the Sheep and the Dragon join together, the Dragon will be the dominant one in the relationship. And in fact, the passive Sheep will welcome the Dragon's leadership wholeheartedly. The Sheep will be attracted to the vibrant and energetic Dragon, and the Dragon will appreciate the creativity and sensitivity in the Sheep. Although sometimes, the Sheep might have problems voicing their frustration, they also hate confrontation and will try to avoid it. In general, this will be a sound and stable relationship, but these two should learn how to bring the best out of each other and keep their communication channel open.

Sheep with Snake 6
This might work

The scheming Snake is the thinker who plans carefully, and the sensitive Sheep is the artist who is creative. They share a love for the arts and the fine things in life. Eventually they will get along because neither of them is comfortable with confrontation. Yet the Snake is often the one in charge between the two, while the Sheep is more than happy to let the Snake take over. In fact, they can probably benefit each other through this union. Nevertheless, the Snake may get tired of the Sheep's sentimental nature, and the Sheep will feel insecurity stemming from the Snake's secretive personality.

Sheep with Horse 8
Good—they won't bore each other

The combination of the Sheep and the Horse will always be exciting. The Horse gives the insecure Sheep confidence and direction and can help the Sheep manage his or her creative talents and business. Disliking sticking to any routine, the couple will live by their own rules. They are both indecisive and, therefore, change their mind constantly. While this trait often annoys people in other animal signs, the Horse and the Sheep understand and tolerate each other. So, this will be quite an interesting couple, and they won't bore each other.

Sheep with Sheep 6
Why not just be friends

Despite the peace-loving nature of the Sheep, the partnership of the double Sheep will be better off as friends than lovers. As both are easygoing and indecisive, the two Sheep will not be competitive over leadership. Neither of them wants to take charge and both avoid responsibilities. Nevertheless, these two do share the same passion for the arts and fine things in life, so if money is not an issue, they will enjoy shopping together for a lavish life. However, their passive nature will prevent them from working toward a successful goal together.

Sheep with Monkey 7
Oh well why not

The union of the Sheep and the Monkey will be stable and calm. The Sheep is attracted to the fun-loving Monkey while the Monkey is inspired by the gentle Sheep's imagination. However, the Sheep is often too dependent, requiring the Monkey to provide constant reassurance; this might put some strain in the relationship. In general, the Monkey needs to know how to comfort the insecure Sheep, and the Sheep needs to learn to let the Monkey move about so he or she won't feel trapped.

Sheep with Rooster 6
They might be unhappy but they'll pretend

The sensitive Sheep and the rigid Rooster are from two different worlds. They have different perspectives on life and move at different speeds. Without a doubt, the Sheep is more relaxed, while the Rooster is diligent and strict. The Rooster will be all work and no play and find the Sheep lazy, and the Sheep will be frustrated by the endless rules set by the Rooster and become resentful. Unhappy as they are, both are unwilling to communicate and resolve their differences. In order to succeed, they must learn to open up and voice their differences and problems.

Sheep with Dog   6
Difficult relationship

The combination of the Sheep and the Dog spells difficulty. The Sheep is very dependent and demands that the Dog provide all of their attention and dedication. Fortunately, the Dog is very tolerant and sympathetic, and will try his or her very best to fulfill the Sheep's wishes. However, the Sheep will keep testing the limit of the Dog's tolerance, eventually bringing out the negative traits of the Dog. In the end, both the Sheep and the Dog will find each other irritating.

Sheep with Pig   9
One of the happiest possible combinations

Congratulations! The Sheep-Pig couple is probably one of the happiest combinations in Chinese astrology. Both are sociable and sensitive, and share much in common and appreciate each other dearly. This couple has a mutual understanding and can benefit a great deal from each other's talents and personality. Both seek harmony and a peaceful life, they don't argue much, and will usually sort out their problems in a calm and reasonable way. Just a little reminder for the couple: Be more conservative with your spending and your lavish lifestyle.

THE FIVE ELEMENTS:
The Sheep—the natural element is Fire

THE METAL SHEEP: 1871, 1931, 1991

The Metal element strengthens the Sheep's artistic taste and talents. Sheep are usually shy and sensitive people, but the Metal increases their determination and confidence. The Metal Sheep, like most Sheep, like to project an image of a brave and confident individual, but deep down, they are just softies who are vulnerable and insecure. Metal Sheep are very artistic, their houses are usually the kind featured in interior design magazines, and Metal Sheep love to show off their good taste. Their social life might not be as busy as the Monkey's or the Snake's, but Metal Sheep feel most comfortable when they are near their own circle of friends. Security and harmony are important to them, so the Metal Sheep usually don't adapt well to changes.

THE WATER SHEEP: 1883, 1943, 2003

The Water element combined with the natural Fire element makes the Water Sheep incredibly sensitive people. Very popular and appealing to others, many try hard to be in their circle of friends. The Water Sheep is opportunistic and knows to seek out people to trust and rely on. These Sheep can be very emotional yet somewhat conservative in projecting their feelings. Diversified and insecure, the Water Sheep fears change and prefers to keep the status quo to ensure his or her security and stability.

THE WOOD SHEEP: 1895, 1955, 2015

The Wood element brings extra creativity and innovation into the already talented Sheep personality, enabling the Wood Sheep to be even more artistic than other Sheep. As thoughtful and sensitive individuals, they are always considerate of others and anxious to please. These loving Sheep have complete trust in dear friends and family, and sometimes even though they know it, they still let people take advantage of them. Wood Sheep have big hearts and always feel for those who are less fortunate. Their compassion will lead them to devote time and money to charity.

THE FIRE SHEEP: 1907, 1967, 2027

As with most Fire types, Fire Sheep are attractive and appealing people. The double-Fire elements heighten their creativity and intuition. Therefore, the Fire Sheep is usually more courageous than others and yet still dependent at times. They know how to emphasize their strength and disguise their weakness well. This type of Sheep is very intelligent and like most Sheep, very artistic. Sheep are never that good at managing their money and Fire Sheep top them all on this one. The Fire Sheep desire to live a lavish life and want to indulge themselves in luxury. On the negative side, Fire Sheep have the tendency to be reckless and often act before they have the chance to think clearly.

THE EARTH SHEEP: 1859, 1919, 1979

The Earth element helps Sheep become more practical and bring their dreamy minds down from the clouds. As with most Earth types, Earth Sheep are cautious and conservative with money; but don't worry, it is not to the extent that they will turn into unpopular Scrooges. In fact, like most Sheep, Earth Sheep enjoy a material life, but will be able to fulfill their own needs without depending too much on others. In general, this is the type of Sheep who plays hard and works hard and is very loyal to friends and family.

The Merry Monkey

Ranking order   **Ninth**

YEARS			ELEMENTS
1908 Feb.02	–	1909 Jan.21	Earth
1920 Feb.20	–	1921 Feb.07	Metal
1932 Feb.06	–	1933 Jan.25	Water
1944 Jan.25	–	1945 Feb.12	Wood
1956 Feb.12	–	1957 Jan.30	Fire
1968 Jan.30	–	1969 Feb.16	Earth
1980 Feb.16	–	1981 Feb.04	Metal
1992 Feb.04	–	1993 Jan.22	Water
2004 Jan.22	–	2005 Feb.08	Wood
2016 Feb.08	–	2017 Jan.27	Fire
2028 Jan.26	–	2029 Feb.12	Earth

Force: Yang
Natural element: Metal
Season and principal month: Summer—August
Direction of its sign: West 30–Southwest 60 degrees
Hours ruled by: 3P.M.–5P.M.
Best companions: Dragon, Rat
Worst companions: Tiger, Snake, Pig
Color: Yellow

PERSONALITY CHARACTERISTICS

Positive	Negative
Altruistic	Arrogant
Candid	Cunning
Charming	Deceitful
Cooperative	Fickle
Creative	Immature
Entertaining	Indifferent
Enthusiastic	Insecure
Generous	Manipulative
Gregarious	Overoptimistic
Independent	Restless
Individualistic	Scheming
Intelligent	Secretive
Inventive	Selfish
Loving	Unfaithful
Optimistic	Unpredictable
Original	
Sensitive	
Sociable	
Vivacious	
Wise	

MONKEY—THE ANIMAL

The most famous Monkey in Chinese literature is probably the *Monkey King*. This is one of the most well known classical novels in Chinese history, and is also known as *Journey to the West*.

The novel is actually based on the true story of a famous Chinese monk, Xuan Zang (602–664) who traveled on foot all the way to India and finally brought back the Buddhist holy book. *Monkey King* is the mythical story of the journey mingled with folk legends, fairy tales, superstitions, monster stories, Taoism, and Buddhism.

When you read the story, you'll know this Monkey King is no ordinary monkey. Born out of a rock, he is witty, inventive, and capable, yet at times, he can be extremely capricious and mischievous. *Monkey King* stole and learned all kinds of magic, tricks, and Gong Fu from masters and Buddhism. And like most action heroes, he has his own vehicle. It is not Batman's Batmobile, nor is it the James Bond's BMW; instead, the Monkey King can travel to the other side of the world in a blink of an eye on his own cloud. And best of all, he'd learned the magic to transform himself into seventy-two different forms such as a mosquito, a rock, or a flea to hide in his enemy's belly to fight the enemy inside out.

MONKEY PEOPLE

Like Monkey King himself, Monkey people are born under the sign of fantasy. You are witty, capable, and eager to learn new things. Usually possessing an above-average intelligence, you have a clever, hyperactive and strong-minded personality. You are always hungry for knowledge and can excel at school. Your talents shine through your childhood and can certainly help you make a name for yourself at a tender age. Go find that high-school yearbook of yours. You will probably remember the old good times when you were a cheerleader or an editor for the school newspaper, or perhaps you were a member of the school football team or the unbeatable debate team. Any teacher could easily tell Monkey students from others because they are usually more energetic, funny, and full of creative and innovative ideas.

Furthermore, if you look into the mirror, you will also see that most Monkey people are quite attractive. And, you are not only smart, but also have a good sense of humor. No wonder you are also very popular! At parties, you'll often find yourself being the center of attention. Actually, everyone knows that you Monkey people love to be in the limelight. Unlike the mysterious Dragons, who draw curious eyes and whispers, your charm and humor wins you popularity in public gatherings or in the clubs.

Monkey people are conversationalists, and yes, you love to talk and talk. But luckily, your creative and original personality prevents you from boring those around you to death. In fact, you are an excellent storyteller—you can transform an ordinary dull biography into a thrilling action story. And your vivid narrative will keep your audience at the edge of their seats for the next three hours, without requesting any snack break!

You are famous for your creativity and invention. You could also turn that boring biography into a musical production. Better yet, you'll invite everyone to see the show for free! That is how talented, creative, and generous you Monkey people are. You are such a good talker that you are always in the winner's circle when debating. Your manner is so friendly and self-assured that people like talking to you. Accordingly, Monkey people feel comfortable speaking in public and are excellent candidates for careers in politics, public relations, and teaching.

Monkeys adore victory, and you love all kinds of challenges. In fact, no challenge is too great for Monkey people. And because of your popularity, stamina, and intelligence, you often become the leader in your community. It's no fun for your rival to fight for the same leadership position against a Monkey opponent. You can be cunning and manipulative sometimes, and you know exactly how to get the votes you need to win the race.

Nevertheless, you are compassionate and friendly, kind and candid, and you can light up the room with your sunshine smile. Always surrounded by friends, you are never short of admirers. No party can be complete without a Monkey guest because you know how to entertain and love to do so. Sociable and diplomatic as you may appear, you can be deceptive sometimes—you hide your opinions of others beneath your apparent friendliness. But even though you are good at hiding your opinions, you have no intention of hiding your emotions. Everyone can tell how you are feeling from miles away— you want everyone to know how happy or depressed you are.

Monkeys have excellent memory, and you are also especially good at problem solving. Anyone who's got a problem can just pick up the phone and call a Monkey friend immediately. Monkey people know how to listen closely and work out solutions at the same time.

Your curiosity causes you to have a great thirst for knowledge. Still, you have few scruples. You can be unreasonable sometimes, and you have the ability to persuade yourself and everyone around you to believe that you are doing the right thing. Some people say that Monkeys are self-centered, some say you are opportunistic, some say you are guileful, but let them say whatever they want—you simply could not care less. You're indifferent to the opinions of others.

People born in the year of Monkey have a good chance of becoming famous. Whatever you do, your charm and luck will make you successful. As a friend, you are loyal and devoted; as a lover, you can be passionate and yet flighty, falling in love easily but tiring of the relationship and quickly looking for another.

Most Monkeys have one fetish—food. But you don't eat like pigs, stuffing yourself with tons of food. Instead, you just have this habit of eating snacks whenever and wherever you like. And here is one more truth about Monkey people like you: You adore bananas! Look in your kitchen, it's probably well stocked with bananas.

THE MALE MONKEY

The male Monkey is the Monkey King himself. He is very clever, astute, and audacious. In his view, he is the center of his own universe. He can make his own rules and break them anytime he chooses.

Always full of energy, he can wake up at 5 A.M., play golf for four hours, go to work and sit through meetings for another six hours, drive two hours to the next city to give a presentation, and then return in time to dance the night away with his friends till 3 A.M. Sometimes, those around him can't help but wonder where he gets all his energy. He is blessed with good health, strength, and an ever-youthful look. He is not the muscular type; nevertheless, he enjoys watching and playing sports. After all, there is no better way for him to get rid of the extra energy he was born with, right? The male Monkey is usually good-looking, and knows just how to use it to his advantage. He may not resemble Tom Cruise, and he is definitely not a pretty boy, but his confidence and charm make him seem even more attractive than Harrison Ford.

The male Monkey relates well to women. As a great entertainer, he knows how to please women, and his great conversation skills allow him to say the right thing at the right moment. The girlfriend of a Monkey man will have lots of fun with her Monkey lover. His quick wit and humor will always make her laugh, and his generosity will shower her with creative presents and surprises. Sounds like a Prince Charming, doesn't he? Not exactly. The male monkey can be fickle and immature. He needs a lot of breathing space and his kingdom to rule. This man is very opinionated, and he seldom listens to others' opinions.

Even though the male Monkeys are charming gentlemen, very few of them end up in the chapel. After all, the grass is always greener on the other side, and it takes more than love and patience to tame this fickle Monkey King. He will never give up his freedom easily. But his lovers shouldn't give up on him. If they love their Monkey man, they should be sure to give him enough room and space to roam around. The truth is that once a Monkey King is tamed, he will make a splendid romantic partner and will look forward to starting a family. As a friend, the male Monkey is very loyal. Although he doesn't trust easily, and will only let his guard down with people he can rely on, once he invites you into his circle, you'll have a good friend for life. Men born under this sign enjoy helping others and possess amazing talents in solving problems—in fact, he sees any dilemma as a challenge to his intelligence. When someone is in trouble, sometimes they don't even need to ask him for help; he will insist on helping so he can prove to himself and everyone that he can find a solution for your problem.

Maybe because of his passion for challenges, the male Monkey also likes to gamble. Since he can lie cheerfully and with extreme confidence, it is hard to figure out if he's bluffing or not, so eventually he comes out as a winner. However, when luck is not on his side, you will probably find him hiding at home for weeks, calculating his debts and counting his remaining dimes.

Always hungry for speed, the male Monkey takes great pleasure and pride in his vehicle. He loves to own a quality car or as many cars as he can afford; BMW, Jaguar, Jeep, or sports cars are definitely some of the top choices on his list.

Playful as he is, the Monkey King focuses his child-like curiosity on everything. There is hardly a dull moment with a male Monkey. So, why not just sit back, relax, and let the Monkey King entertain with his charm and humor?

THE FEMALE MONKEY

Attractive and sensitive, the female Monkey is popular and very much in demand. Her playful sense of humor crowns her as the prom queen wherever she goes, and her lively personality wins her a wide circle of friends and acquaintances.

Self-assured and sensitive, the Monkey woman knows how to present the best side of herself. Knowing the proper things to say at the right time, she is comfortable even while making fun of herself. Her jokes are rarely hurtful or mean; they most likely reflect the silliness she sees in everything. At times, the Monkey woman can be flirtatious, and when her mischievous side surfaces, she enjoys provoking jealousy among her admirers and watching the fireworks.

The Monkey woman is a show-off who knows how to attract attention to herself. She is hungry for knowledge and is extremely competitive and resourceful. Wherever she goes, she can stir up excitement and dazzle people with her liveliness and charm. This is probably why many Monkey women have been attracted to the stage lights and are famous performers in show business. Stars like Elizabeth Taylor and Diana Ross are two.

The Monkey woman is so intuitive she can read someone like a book with her keen observation. An excellent mentor and a patient listener, the Monkey woman is also a superb problem-solver. If you want your Monkey lady friend to solve your problem, get in line behind the dozen other friends waiting to hear her insight and original solutions. She is extremely loyal to her friends and more honest than the male Monkey in many ways.

However, like the male Monkey, the Monkey woman is an independent individual. She needs to have her own space, her own stage, and she knows exactly what she wants in life. Practical and calculating, she will not work for free. In fact, she counts her dollars and cents carefully and is saving up her pennies for her own grand plan.

As a lover, this Monkey woman is warm, loving, creative, and spontaneous. A relationship with her might be like a roller coaster, filled with romance, passion, laughter, fights, tears, and reconciliation. But just like a trip to the action theme park, you will enjoy every moment of the thrill, the ups and downs and the excitement.

The female Monkey doesn't easily commit to a relationship. Only constant stimulation will keep the relationship lively and interesting. Opinionated and critical she may be, because she's cautious when it comes to choosing her lifetime partner. Nevertheless, once a Monkey lady decides to settle down, she will be a devoted wife and mother. Loving, fun, and tolerant, she is good with children, usually having lots of them, and can organize her family well.

Most Monkey women are good with their hands. She could be an exceptional pianist, a gourmet cook, a sculptor, or a handywoman. Her born curiosity and quest for knowledge enable her to master any profession she chooses. Practical and capable, Monkey women can be do-it-yourself geniuses. This lady doesn't wait for her Prince Charming to rescue her when something breaks; in fact, she will roll up her sleeves, get her own tools and a good how-to book, and fix the problem in about ten minutes.

As a caring, amusing, resourceful, and charming companion, the female Monkey is one of a kind and should never be underestimated.

MONKEY AT WORK

With their intelligence and popularity, Monkey people can succeed in any profession. Monkeys are versatile and smart people who can find work wherever they are. Their knowledge, resourcefulness, and love of facing any challenge put in front of them make them assets to any company.

As a boss, Monkey is a generous leader who encourages brainstorming and gives their staff room to learn and improve. This Monkey boss enjoys directing people and can be demanding sometimes. Opinionated as they are, Monkey Queens and Kings will not allow other opinions and can be overambitious and impatient at times.

As an employee, the Monkey is calculating, creative, gregarious, and audacious, and will work day and night to prove his or her capability to superiors. Talkative and witty enough to know just the right way to persuade customers or clients makes the Monkey a hell of a salesperson. They could probably sell a refrigerator to an Eskimo and convince him it's a collector's item as well as an attractive piece of furniture.

As a business partner, Monkey is an exceptional negotiator. They are gifted talkers and know how to use their talent to their advantage. Occasionally they can be cunning and mischievous, and unwelcoming of advice from others. Another problem with Monkey partners is that sometimes they may get carried away, do everything, and leave nothing for their partners to do.

As a colleague, Monkeys are sociable, charming, and fun. They always know how to lighten up a tense moment and enjoy playing harmless pranks on their coworkers. Although they can be controlling at times, it is simply because they truly believe that it is the best and most efficient way for everyone.

Monkeys thrive in creative fields. They hate routine and will feel trapped in a predictable career. So if you want to retain your talented Monkey employees, you must constantly provide them with challenges. Assign a variety of tasks, then give them the room to be innovative. Monkeys are at their best when utilizing their wits and creativity.

Nevertheless, some Monkeys don't like to settle down with one job. Working as a freelancer or a consultant may be best in order to have their freedom as well as the challenge. Moreover, some Monkeys tend to jump from one career to another. They are adventurous, confident, and believe they can do anything. So, a Monkey starts as an editor for a publishing company, then the next year, performs in a Broadway show, and then moves on to the next job as a diving coach.

BEST MONKEY OCCUPATIONS

Art critic	Movie star
Bus driver	Nurse
Clerk	Politician
Counselor	Reporter
Diplomat	Stockbroker
English teacher	Theologian
Foreign correspondent	Therapist
Installation artist	Town planner
Journalist	Vocalist
Judo instructor	Writer
Editor	

FAMOUS MONKEYS

Charles Dickens	Julius Caesar
Danny DeVito	Leonardo da Vinci
David Copperfield	Michael Douglas
Diana Ross	Tom Hanks
Elizabeth Taylor	Tom Selleck
James Stewart	Will Smith
Jennifer Aniston	

COMPATIBILITY

The Chinese believe each animal sign is most compatible with signs that are four years apart, and least compatible with the sign that is six years apart. Based on this concept, a circle can be drawn with all signs, locating the Triangle of Affinity and the Circle of Conflict.

TRIANGLE OF AFFINITY
Monkey, Rat, Dragon are the Triangle of Affinity

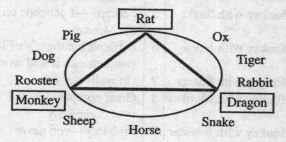

CIRCLE OF CONFLICT
Monkey's conflict sign is Tiger

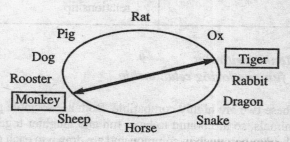

Signs	Rating 1–10	Relationship
Monkey with Rat	9	A fun and loving relationship
Monkey with Ox	8	Nice—they are compatible and stable
Monkey with Tiger	*3*	*Better stay away from each other*
Monkey with Rabbit	7	Amusing relationship
Monkey with Dragon	8	This might work—they admire each other
Monkey with Snake	5	Perhaps—it depends on the Monkey
Monkey with Horse	6	Difficult but there's still a small chance it will work
Monkey with Sheep	7	Oh well why not
Monkey with Monkey	8	Great companions and total complicity
Monkey with Rooster	7	Probably—you never know
Monkey with Dog	6	With reservations—the Dog might suffer
Monkey with Pig	6	Not a balanced relationship

Monkey with Rat   9
A fun and loving relationship

These two are highly compatible. Both are sociable party animals, so are bound to have fun and laughter together. The duo has much in common and are drawn to each other by their mutual interests and talents. They admire each other for their intelligence and creativity and share the same values and attitude. They are more likely to dine out a lot because they have too many friends to hang out with. On the whole, although this relationship can be emotional at times, there will be no dull moments. The Rat should learn to accept the Monkey's dominance and this will be a lasting, intriguing, and one of the best relationships.

Monkey with Ox   8
Nice—they are compatible and stable

At the beginning, these two have plenty of laughter—the mischievous Monkey enjoys teasing the serious Ox, and the Monkey's charm and lively personality fascinates the Ox. But gradually, the sparks fade away, and the reserved Ox will have difficulty understanding the capricious Monkey and will not always approve of the Monkey's way of doing things. Similarly, the restless Monkey will not be patient enough to sit around and wait for the overcautious and inflexible Ox to change. These two will have difficulty understanding or changing for each other, but the optimistic Monkey knows how to eventually cheer up the Ox.

Monkey with Tiger   3
Better stay away from each other

Monkey and Tiger are both competitive and refuse to compromise. As both of them are proud and intelligent, the Tiger may be easily offended by the Monkey's remarks, and the Monkey may not have the patience for Tiger's explosive temper. These two will fight and retaliate, and will always be on guard for the next possible provocation. The Tiger, which is six years apart from the

Monkey, is the sign of conflict for the Monkey. What more can be said except that you two are definitely not meant for each other?

Monkey with Rabbit 7
Amusing relationship

These two don't have much in common. Monkey thinks the shrewd Rabbit is dull and boring, while the Rabbit finds it hard to trust the cunning and fickle Monkey. However, these two will not confront each other head to head like the Monkey and Ox, nor will they retaliate like the Tiger and Monkey. Instead, they will leave the door of communication open and wait for the right time to negotiate a way to work things out. Although this relationship might work, it will be somewhat distant and tolerant.

Monkey with Dragon 8
This might work—they admire each other

Monkey and Dragon are one of the best of combinations. Both powerful and intelligent, they communicate on the same level and share the same vision and interests. Both have good instincts, are affectionate, and know exactly how to handle and please the other. Overall, whether in love or in business relationships, Monkey and Dragon make a successful team together.

Monkey with Snake 5
Perhaps—it depends on the Monkey

At the beginning, these two find each other mysterious and intriguing, but the attraction will quickly wear off, and they will start finding faults in each other. Sometimes the Snake can't tolerate the mischievous and cunning Monkey show-off. Likewise, the Monkey will get tired of the enigmatic Snake, who tends to keep his or her thoughts to himself or herself—"Talk to me!" the Monkey will say. Communication will become a problem, and the relationship might be rocky.

Monkey with Horse   6
Difficult but there's still a small chance it will work

The Monkey and the Horse will get along fine with each other most of the time. Because they are both flexible and accepting, they won't be struggling for dominance and can cooperate and solve any conflict that occurs. However, the Monkey may feel insecure around the restless and impatient Horse. And the Horse's inability to open up will bring tension between these two and cause communication problems. If these two can find their pace and rhythm and work things out, there might still be a chance of success for their union.

Monkey with Sheep   7
Oh well why not

The union of the Monkey and the Sheep will be stable and calm. The Sheep is attracted to the fun-loving Monkey while the Monkey is inspired by the gentle Sheep's imagination. Often too dependent, the Sheep requires the Monkey to provide constant reassurance, and this might put some strain on the relationship. Generally speaking, the Monkey needs to know how to comfort the insecure Sheep, and the Sheep needs to learn to leave room for the Monkey to move about so the Monkey will not feel trapped.

Monkey with Monkey   8
Great companions and total complicity

When you put two Monkeys in a room, you are bound to
hear laughter, genius ideas, and, yes, argument, too. Both
talented and resourceful, the two-Monkey union is a very
powerful team if they can put their heads together.
However, there might be some struggles for dominance,
and jealousy—after all, there can only be one Monkey
King under one roof. Fortunately, these two are smart
enough to know how to communicate and can always resolve any differences or problems. When the two form a
family, with their creative, humorous, and sparkling personalities, this will definitely be quite a fun house.

Monkey with Rooster   7
Probably—you never know

The Monkey and the Rooster can get along. When they
first meet, the attraction is powerful, but gradually they
will see the differences and learn to work around them.
Being the philosopher of the two, Roosters usually keep
too many thoughts to themselves and avoid confrontation, while the merry Monkey desires to communicate openly. Eventually, these two will learn to respect
their differences, find the balance, and develop a
workable relationship based on their interests.

Monkey with Dog   6
With reservations—the Dog might suffer

These two seem like a perfect match for each other; one
possesses qualities lacking in the other. And, this union

can actually produce great friends. The truth is, the Dog is easygoing and kind, and the sociable and lively Monkey can be both charming and manipulative. Wanna guess who takes the dominance in the relationship? The pessimistic Dog will let the Monkey take control and lead the way, but will expect the flirtatious and fickle Monkey to be loyal and honest in the relationship. Although love is possible between these two, the Dog might be disappointed and suffer.

Monkey with Pig   6
Not a balanced relationship

Both are optimistic and friendly, both are popular and sociable. The Monkey and the Pig could make a great team. In this relationship, they will enjoy each other's company and can always learn and benefit from each other. Hopefully, the Pig won't mind the Monkey's plans and schemes, and the Monkey will be able to help and support the Pig. As long as they have the same vision and interest, these two can make great friends and lovers.

THE FIVE ELEMENTS:
The Monkey—the natural element is Metal

THE METAL MONKEY: 1860, 1920, 1980

Metal is the Monkey's natural element; therefore, a person born in the year of Metal Monkey becomes a double-Metal Monkey. The double-metal multiplies Monkey's intelligence, but also increases the aggressiveness. This is the fighting Monkey.

Usually strong and independent, Metal Monkeys like to run their own business and be their own bosses. They love money and all the material things they can afford, and fortunately, they are capable of making smart investments, often making a lot of money from their talents.

Metal Monkeys are gamblers, and frustratingly to others, they always end up the winners. However, these Monkeys also realize the importance of saving for rainy days. On the negative side, Metal Monkeys are proud and self-conscious, and are usually only loyal to themselves.

THE WATER MONKEY: 1872, 1932, 1992

Water mates well with Monkey's natural element, Metal. Together they produce a harmonious combination that brings sensitivity and compassion to the Water Monkey. Usually kind and understanding, Water Monkey can sometimes be too sensitive and take things too personally.

Secretive at times, Water Monkeys have the tendency to hide their true feelings within themselves and can become evasive. Nevertheless, they are popular among friends because they possess a keen sense of how human relationships function.

THE WOOD MONKEY: 1884, 1944, 2004

The Wood-Metal combination makes the Wood Monkey creative and lucky. People born as the Wood Monkey are very good at interpersonal communication. They are usually observant and aware of everything that is going on around them.

The Wood element helps focus and stabilize Monkey people, and makes them natural leaders and innovators.

These Monkeys are very resourceful, creative, and excellent problem-solvers. They are always curious and searching for answers and will not take setbacks easily.

THE FIRE MONKEY: 1869, 1956, 2016

The Fire Monkey is the most forceful of all Monkeys. They are full of life, and always appear vital, powerful, and aggressive. Self-assured and determined, they always end up at the top of their chosen professions. The Fire Monkey is passionate, expressive, and very interested in the opposite sex. Nevertheless, the Fire-Metal combination also brings conflict to the Fire Monkeys. These Monkeys have great potential but do not seem to see their own limitations and sometimes end up overreaching themselves.

THE EARTH MONKEY: 1908, 1968, 2028

The Earth element supplies the calmness to the Monkey's natural Metal nature. Less concerned about their ego, Earth Monkeys are more honest and sympathetic than the other Monkey people. Generally, they are highly intelligent and always hungry for knowledge; moreover, they are patient and scientific in their approach to problem solving. This is probably why Earth Monkeys enjoy pursuing higher education and even end up as famous scholars and researchers.

On the downside, Earth Monkeys can be harsh and too blunt with their criticisms, which can increase tension in their personal relationships.

The Enthusiastic Rooster

Ranking order   Tenth

YEARS		ELEMENTS
1909 Jan.22	– 1910 Feb.18	Earth
1921 Feb.08	– 1922 Jan.27	Metal
1933 Jan.26	– 1934 Feb.13	Water
1945 Feb.13	– 1946 Feb.01	Wood
1957 Jan.31	– 1958 Feb.17	Fire
1969 Feb.17	– 1970 Feb.05	Earth
1981 Feb.05	– 1982 Jan.24	Metal
1993 Jan.23	– 1994 Feb.09	Water
2005 Feb.09	– 2006 Jan.28	Wood
2017 Jan.28	– 2018 Feb.15	Fire
2029 Feb.13	– 2030 Feb.01	Earth

Force:	Yin
Natural element:	Metal
Season and principal month:	Autumn—September
Direction of its sign:	Direct West +30 and -30 degrees
Hours ruled by:	5 P.M.–7 P.M.
Best companions:	Ox, Snake
Worst companions:	Rat, Rabbit, Rooster, Dog
Color:	Yellow, White

PERSONALITY CHARACTERISTICS

Positive	Negative
Adventurous	Argumentative
Attractive	Arrogant
Brave	Boastful
Capable	Cranky
Charitable	Critical
Charming	Cynical
Communicative	Dissipated
Courageous	Self-absorbed
Entertaining	Self-involved
Enthusiastic	Self-preoccupied
Funny	Superior
Generous	Thoughtless
Hardworking	Too egotistical
Honest	Vain
Loyal	Vulnerable
Passionate	
Prompt	
Relaxed	
Sincere	
Thoughtful	

ROOSTER—THE ANIMAL

Roosters are morning birds. The legend is that originally Roosters were stars fallen to earth and given the responsibility to crow on time every morning to wake humans.

In China, the Rooster is associated with five virtues. Its crown represents confidence; its claws represent dexterity in sports; its daily morning crow indicates trust-worthiness and military honor; its never-back-down-from-an-enemy nature symbolizes courage; and its willingness to divide food with others signifies kindness.

Many believe if one desires to succeed, one must learn from the Rooster and be consistent and hardworking. There is a famous idiom called "Exercise at Cock's Crow." It is a story about two young men that were both determined to render service to their country. One late night, they were inspired and awakened by an early cock's crow and decided to study every day at the first sound of the crow. Eventually, both become generals of the Jin Dynasty and won many battles for the country.

ROOSTER PEOPLE

Born under the sign of frankness, you are very intelligent and educated. You are the thinker, the philosopher, and the observant. You see things in black and white, and, most of the time, you are quite accurate and precise with your observations. Sometimes people wonder if you were born with an invisible eye in the back of your head. Perhaps this is why many believe that you have a sixth sense.

Just like a true Rooster, who shows off his gorgeous feathers, you like to be noticed and flattered. As one of the most misunderstood and eccentric of all signs, you might dress a little flashily compared to others, but in your heart, you are completely conservative and old-fashioned. You are quite attractive, and you take pride in your looks and style. Appearance is really important to you, and you certainly know how to dress up. However, because you are never satisfied, you are constantly improving yourself. Acknowledging the latest fashion but never blindly following it, you make your own fashion statement through variations and individuality. In reality you are a little too obsessed with your looks—not many people can spend as many hours standing in front of the mirrors as you do. Moreover, you can easily spend hundreds of dollars for a dress without hesitation. Of course, this doesn't mean you don't care about money; you love to compare prices and are always happy to find even the smallest bargain.

You have a colorful personality and are considered flamboyant. Fortunately, you often make quite a good impression where you go. With Roosters, it is strictly "what you see is what you get." There are no hidden depths to the Rooster's character. Neither complicated nor profound, you are very forthright and straightforward. You are quite persuasive and enjoy debate and lively discussion. You don't mind sharing your opinions with others, and sometimes, even though you don't intend it, you can be a bit tactless and hurtful. When facing authority, you never back down easily and often stand up for what you believe. Although you don't like to admit it, you are actually quite arrogant and self-absorbed at times. You see everyone's shortcomings but yours and have high standards for yourself and those around you. A born perfectionist, you often pick on others more than you do yourself.

Some criticize you for being overconfident and shortsighted. And you know that part of that criticism is quite true. You do believe that you know best and often listen to no one but yourself. Easily anxious and aggressive, you have the determination and patience to achieve your goal and give it time and consistency. These will be the tickets to great success you've longed for.

Believe it or not, it is not an easy task to fool the Rooster. Your mind is cautious and skeptical; using your perceptive gift makes you an excellent troubleshooter, detective, doctor, nurse, and psychiatrist. Enthusiastic about what you do, you can be quite a pushover but have zero tolerance for sloppiness. Hardworking, resourceful, courageous and multitalented, you are always up, out and doing. One rarely sees a relaxed Rooster sitting quietly in the living room, doing nothing. You can find many different paths to accomplishment.

Though sharp, practical, and resourceful, like people born in the year of the Sheep, you also like to dream. You have the tendency to think big and fantasize. This daydreaming can cause you to lose sight of reality and eventually disappoint your loved one. After all, reality will never match up to the dreams you have in mind.

You make a great host and adore entertaining. You are quite famous for your people skills and ensure that everyone feels at ease. Indeed, there will be no quiet dinners at home for the Rooster on Friday night; it is more fun to go dancing with friends or shopping at the mall.

Emotionally, you are very passionate but often fear personal commitment when it comes to serious relationships. Aside from honesty, the main virtue in the Rooster character is loyalty: You are a devoted and trustworthy friend. You always keep your promises and are always true to your word. When a Rooster loves and admires someone, he or she will bend over backward or even catch the moon just to keep the other person happy.

Overall, on the good side, you are distinguished, intelligent, and courageous, and are very likely to be successful owing to your diligent nature. But on the downside, you can be too self-assured and boastful, and you can be easily fooled by compliments and sweet words and do not take well to criticisms. In addition, you need to learn that looks aren't everything. And utilizing your excellent people skills and organized mind, you should try to be less boastful and dreamy and focus on the doable and the reality.

THE MALE ROOSTER

Like the bird itself, male Roosters are quite attractive. Often dressed in fine and expensive clothes, the Rooster man likes to show off, swagger, and attract the attention of the opposite sex. He loves being in the company of women and is entertaining and witty. This charming man often knows when and what to say to please the ladies in the room. No wonder he is quite popular among female friends.

He is very opinionated and forms instant judgments about someone on sight. Honesty is his virtue and sometimes can also be his fault. He can be honest about how he feels but also brutally frank about how ugly he thinks you look in that pink dress you wore especially for him. It is not that he is insensitive; it is only that he believes the best way to interact with people is simply by telling the truth, bluntly.

He takes great pride in his education, is quite good at languages, and always loves a good and harmless debate. Talkative at times, he enjoys serious discussion and likes to exchange ideas and opinions on issues. Tidy and organized, Rooster man can often be found carrying a personal digital assistant to help him sort schedules, appointments, and thoughts.

Although appearing indifferent, he is actually very ebullient at heart. He values his public image and tries everything to maintain it. Although sometimes self-centered and stubborn, he is generally liked among his friends. Often attracted to large social functions, the Rooster man enjoys attending weddings and big parties. After all, this is the best opportunity for him to be in the spotlight and show off his beautiful crown and feathers.

He is quite a detailed and quick thinker. He enjoys observing from outside looking into any situation and is considered a tremendous problem-solver. Family and friends value his advice and suggestions and are often amazed by his accuracy in prediction.

However, he refuses to take anyone's advice in return and listens to no one but himself. Aggressive and ambitious, the Rooster man can be unrealistic in his goals and this may create bumps in his road to success. A true perfectionist, he likes to be in control and is quite critical of others' faults. He does not make decisions easily and prefers to weigh things from every possible angle before making the final decision.

In love relationships, the Rooster man is proud and emotional. Passionate and captivating, this Rooster man has one busy love life despite his quite dominating, thoughtless, and somewhat chauvinistic manner. But when another man is too close to his lady, this proud Rooster man sees nothing but jealous green, and can be extremely cocky and unreasonable. In general, he needs to be less cynical and critical in the heat of an argument and learn how to communicate better with others.

THE FEMALE ROOSTER

The female Rooster is sociable and communicative. She is usually physically attractive and good at details. Stylish and well dressed, this female Rooster does not show up with flashy clothes as much as the Rooster man does. Prudent and careful, she is very good at managing other people's money; however, when it comes to shopping for clothes, this Rooster woman suddenly loses all sense of money and figures. She will buy a gorgeous coat without thinking twice despite its price. Nevertheless, Rooster lady loves any kind of bargain. To a female Rooster, her appearance is the main source of her strong confidence. She can spend hours before going out to a party, not because she is as indecisive as a Sheep woman, who is unsure about what to wear, but because this Rooster lady plans things ahead and knows exactly what color she will wear for the occasion. Nevertheless, she can tirelessly spend three hours doing her face and hair.

Considerate and sensitive, she has many friends. Often a great listener and adviser, many knock on her door for guidance and suggestions. She often hangs out with her girlfriends in her very loyal circle. Unable to tell even white lies, the Rooster woman is very trustworthy. While she can be a little bit malicious, she is very well liked for her down to earth personality. Outgoing, outspoken, and obliging, her many good qualities include honesty, reliability, and trustworthiness.

Romantically, the female Rooster is very passionate and sincere, and never short of suitors. Although she is not as controlling as the male Rooster, she is secretly a jealous person and can't let anything stand between her and her lover. Honor and honesty are very important to her, and she is a lady who will keep her promises no matter what. For those of you who are dating a Rooster lady, try to be supportive whenever she needs you and avoid agitating her with unnecessary argument and jealousy.

The Rooster woman applies herself totally to whatever she does. She is very astute and observant and is usually quite successful in her career and well respected among her colleagues and friends. Naturally tidy and organized, she likes to keep everything neat. These kinds of talents make her the perfect candidate to organize a big social event or a work conference.

ROOSTER AT WORK

Usually, Roosters are not blessed by good fortune; instead, they have to work hard to achieve success. Diligent and hardworking, Roosters are aggressive and ambitious when it comes to their careers. They are self-assured people and possess powerful personalities. Born organizers, they are refined and tidy-minded. Needless to say, they like to keep everything neat, and they plan ahead. If you have the chance to check out a Rooster friend's room or office, you will discover that the desk of a Rooster is usually quite neat; things are in their proper place and documents are systematically filed.

At their company, Roosters are likely to be department heads. One of their strengths is finance management, and they are good at it, both personally and professionally. They are prudent with money and suited for jobs as accountants and bank managers. Roosters can succeed in any profession that requires nerve, self-confidence, and charisma; therefore, they are suited to anything concerned with selling as well as commercial professions. Always ready for a lively discussion, Roosters seems to shine in jobs associated with the media, perhaps on a news-based television show or as a journalist for a newspaper.

Roosters are interested in topical events and dislike routine, with the exception of wearing uniforms. Surprisingly, Roosters like jobs that require wearing uniforms. They love being the authority and take pride in wearing the uniform.

As a boss, the Rooster is authoritative and critical, definitely not the "world's best boss." They can be unrealistic about their goals and, unfortunately, they rarely take advice from anyone else. Therefore, it is sometimes a mission impossible to persuade them out of their naïve and impractical goals. However, it is those who work for them who will have to struggle with the consequences.

As a business partner, they are cautious and careful when it comes to decisions and responsibilities. Though appearing uncommunicative, they need constant stimulation from the partner to reform their business models. Born finance managers, they can be very prudent about the checkbook and fussy and picky on money and figures. They need partners who are equally strong-headed and confident, but not as argumentative.

As a colleague, they are sociable and fun-loving. They crave compliments and thrive under the spotlight. Sometimes, a small compliment can go a long way for this proud Rooster. They are helpful and generous, and definitely not dependent types like the Sheep or the Rabbit. They are observant and always come up with the right solution to any problem. Not surprisingly, people often come to them for their guidance and suggestions. In general, with their analytical skills, philosophical minds, and argumentative natures, Roosters will do well in finance and media. Larry King and Dean Koontz are just two famous Rooster people.

BEST ROOSTER OCCUPATIONS

Actor	Police officer
Artist	Politician
Athlete	Public relations officer
Beautician	Restaurant owner
Critic	Sales director
Dental surgeon	Sales person
Entertainer	Security guard
Farmer	Soldier
Fashion designer	Teacher
Fireman	Travel guide
Hairdresser	Travel writer
Journalist	Waiter
Manicurist	Writer
Newsreader	

FAMOUS ROOSTERS

Chris Carter	Goldie Hawn
Confucius	Johann Strauss
Dean Koontz	Larry King
Dolly Parton	Michelle Pfeiffer
Donny Osmond	Rachmaninoff
Eric Clapton	Roman Polanski
Gloria Estefan	Steffi Graf

COMPATIBILITY

The Chinese believe each animal sign is most compatible with signs that are four years apart, and least compatible with the sign that is six years apart. Based on this concept, a circle can be drawn with all signs, locating the Triangle of Affinity and the Circle of Conflict.

TRIANGLE OF AFFINITY
Rooster, Ox, Snake are the Triangle of Affinity

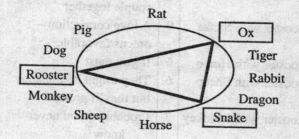

CIRCLE OF CONFLICT
Rooster's sign of conflict is Rabbit

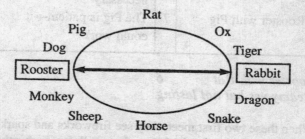

Signs	Rating 1–10	Relationship
Rooster with Rat	6	Steamy yes but not lasting
Rooster with Ox	8	You are lucky to find each other
Rooster with Tiger	6	Not a balanced relationship
Rooster with Rabbit	*5*	*Well maybe not*
Rooster with Dragon	8	You two make a good couple together
Rooster with Snake	9	A love connection— omens favorable
Rooster with Horse	6	If you must
Rooster with Sheep	6	They might be unhappy but they'll pretend
Rooster with Monkey	7	Probably—you never know
Rooster with Rooster	3	It will be a miracle if it works
Rooster with Dog	6	Only if it's absolutely necessary
Rooster with Pig	7	The Pig is patient—it could work

Rooster with Rat   6
Steamy yes but not lasting

When these two first meet, they see fireworks and sparks, but as the steam slowly fades, they will see each other more clearly, and disagreements will start to rise. In this combination, the Rat and Rooster will find themselves in constant debate over who leads. The Rooster can be extremely critical of the Rat, and the sociable Rat will find ways to get even with the Rooster by making the Rooster jealous. Eventually, it will take a lot of effort to keep this relationship alive.

Rooster with Ox   8
You are lucky to find each other

Luckily, the relationship between the Ox and the Rooster will be harmonious and stable. In fact, this combination might be the best match for the Ox. Both signs are well organized and plan ahead, and both care a lot about money and financial security. In this couple, the Rooster will probably be the spokesperson, while the Ox enjoys watching the Rooster show off. They are very compatible, and both sides will benefit from the other's company. Occasionally, the opinionated Rooster should learn to tone down the attitude and resolve the differences.

Rooster with Tiger   6
Not a balanced relationship

Tiger and Rooster do share many things in common. Although the relationship appears promising at first, it will go downhill soon afterward. The Rooster, as a perfectionist, tends to order others to follow his or her rules. This lecturing nature of the Rooster will annoy the independent Tiger and bring out the Tiger's rebellious personality. In general, this doesn't make for a balanced relationship. They are both inclined to pick on the other for his or her faults. Misunderstanding might be one of the biggest issues they have to overcome, but if they share a common interest, they will find ways to patch things up.

Rooster with Rabbit   5
Well maybe not

The differences between these two might eventually undermine this relationship. Both intelligent and witty, the Rooster is a show-off at heart, and the Rabbit simply cannot stand the Rooster's cocky attitude. There will be many misunderstandings and miscommunications between them. The Rabbit might be turned off by the Rooster's never-ending criticism, and the Rooster will find the Rabbit indifferent and insensitive. These two don't seem to communicate in the same channel and often rub each other the wrong way.

Rooster with Dragon   8
You two make a good couple together

The combination of the Dragon and Rooster can be a fine one. The Dragon admires the Rooster's talents and intelligence, while the Rooster appreciates the Dragon's confidence and stamina. Though both can be a little cocky, they will work well together toward a mutual goal, and with their talents and optimism, they will eventually succeed. In the meantime, these two both enjoy being in the limelight, so there might be a time when these two are fighting over it. Nevertheless, they both know not to let their argument get out of hand, so in general these two will make a good couple together.

Rooster with Snake   9
A love connection—omens favorable

This is yet another love connection recommended by the Chinese. The Snake and the Rooster understand and admire each other for their talents and ability. They are both workaholics, and they are both ambitious and focused. The Snake will be the schemer who plans carefully in this partnership, and the Rooster will be the executor who carries out the scheme. Intelligent and capable, this team is bound to succeed when they put their heads together. This will be a loving and balanced relationship.

Rooster with Horse   6
If you must

The witty Horse and the smart Rooster are equal in their intelligence and talents. At the beginning, these two will get along fine, and each one's strengths will complement the other's. However, as time goes by, the impatient Horse might find the Rooster too critical and demanding. At the same time, the Rooster simply cannot understand why the Horse wants to spread him or herself so thin in too many projects and can't seem to remain devoted to or focused on one thing. Once the Rooster shows his or her argumentative nature, the quick-tempered Horse will be annoyed and ready to walk away.

Rooster with Sheep   6
They might be unhappy but they'll pretend

The sensitive Sheep and the rigid Rooster are from two different worlds. They have different perspectives on life and move at different speeds. Without a doubt, the Sheep is laid-back and relaxed, while the Rooster is diligent and strict. The Rooster is all work and no play and will find the Sheep lazy, and the Sheep will be frustrated by the endless rules set by the Rooster and become resentful. Unhappy as they are, both are unwilling to communicate and resolve their differences. In order to succeed, they must learn to open up and voice their differences and problems.

Rooster with Monkey   7
Probably—you never know

The Monkey and the Rooster can enjoy each other's company. When they first meet, the attraction is powerful, but gradually they will see differences between them and will have to learn to work around them. Being the philosopher of the two, the Rooster usually keeps too many thoughts to him or herself to avoid confrontation, while the merry Monkey desires to communicate openly. Eventually, these two will learn to respect their differences, find the right balance, and develop a workable relationship based on their interests.

Rooster with Rooster   3
It will be a miracle if it works

In ancient China, some of the best entertainment in town was the Rooster fights. Therefore, it is no surprise that Roosters will fight most of the time. Two Roosters will share the same positive and negative traits and are less tolerant with the other in the relationship. Both of them are arrogant and critical; these two Roosters can probably argue about anything, anywhere, anytime. The Roosters tend only to see others' faults but are blind to their own. Their endless arguments will make those around them miserable.

Rooster with Dog   6
Only if it's absolutely necessary

The Rooster and the Dog don't always see eye to eye. The Dog usually thinks the Rooster too argumentative and unkind, while the Rooster simply cannot stand the Dog's high moral standards. This will not be a balanced relationship since Roosters will be aggressive and expect the tolerant Dogs to support their every decision. Dogs will try to understand and be supportive, but eventually, their patience will run out, and they will end up apart.

Rooster with Pig   7
The Pig is patient—it could work

The Rooster and the Pig work well together as a couple. The Pig does not mind the Rooster's controlling nature, and the Rooster values the Pig's generosity and sensitivity. These two can be good friends and compatible lovers. There might be some troubles when conflict arrives, due to the Rooster's and the Pig's different approaches to problem solving. Nevertheless, the Pig is very patient and sympathetic, and will put up with the Rooster's criticism and eventually calm him or her down.

THE FIVE ELEMENTS:
The Rooster—the natural element is Metal

THE METAL ROOSTER: 1861, 1921, 1981

The Metal element makes the already headstrong Rooster even more opinionated and stubborn. Double-Metal can sometimes mean extra trouble for the Rooster. They are very organized and pay attention to all the details, but they have extremely high expectations of themselves and others. The passionate and ambitious Metal Roosters are usually workaholics, and are sometimes eager to win fame and wealth. Nevertheless, the Metal Rooster can be completely committed to social work in an attempt to help mankind. On the negative side, Metal Roosters are picky to a fault, and their harsh criticism offends. In addition they often hide their emotions, and if they don't learn how to compromise and relax, their talents could be wasted.

THE WATER ROOSTER: 1873, 1933, 1993

The Water-Metal combination heightens the Water Roosters' intelligence. They are clearheaded and practical, and always know how to seek out and use resources to achieve their goals. The Water Roosters are somewhat obsessed with systems, medicine, and technology. They too often focus on the procedures and details and sometimes lose sight of the "big picture." Water Roosters are sympathetic and win support through persuasion instead of by intimidation. The Water element helps to make the Rooster sensitive and adaptable; Water Roosters are not as authoritarian as other Roosters.

THE WOOD ROOSTER: 1885, 1945, 2005

The Wood element creates a Rooster with high integrity. Much less stubborn than the others, the Wood Rooster can be very considerate and have a wider outlook in life. Social and open-minded, they can be unselfishly devoted to social welfare, and their organized minds also help them excel in their work performance. Nevertheless, a Wood Rooster is still a Rooster, and their high standards still drive everyone crazy and their criticism is always hard to swallow. The Wood Rooster should learn not to overstretch by taking on too many projects.

THE FIRE ROOSTER: 1897, 1957, 2017

The Fire element combined with the Rooster's natural Metal element creates an exceptional individual who is often a great leader, hero, or pioneer. Fire Roosters are people of action; they are vigorous and highly motivated. Always focused and strongly principled, they can single-mindedly pursue their goals and will not be easily moved by others' opinions or feelings. They are very persuasive, which makes them natural leaders and managers, but at times they can be too inflexible to compromise. Nevertheless, the Fire Rooster will always have noble intentions behind their actions and will be successful.

THE EARTH ROOSTER: 1849, 1909, 1969

The analytical Earth Rooster likes to dig for the truth. The Earth Element calms the Earth Roosters and makes them less dramatic and talkative than other Roosters. Earth Roosters are very efficient and can be trusted with a truckload of responsibilities. They are serious about their jobs, taking notes, filing data, and can be very systematic. However, the Earth element makes them shy away from confrontation, and when personal problems occur, they tend to stick their heads into the sand like ostriches. They are philosophical at times and tend to keep their own counsel and not speak up for themselves. But if they do ever speak up, you can be sure their words will be blunt and explosive.

The Dutiful Dog

Ranking order	Eleventh

YEARS			ELEMENTS
1910 Feb.10	–	1911 Jan.29	Metal
1922 Jan.28	–	1923 Feb.15	Water
1934 Feb.14	–	1935 Feb.03	Wood
1946 Feb.02	–	1947 Jan.21	Fire
1958 Feb.18	–	1959 Feb.07	Earth
1970 Feb.06	–	1971 Jan.26	Metal
1982 Jan.25	–	1983 Feb.12	Water
1994 Feb.10	–	1995 Jan.30	Wood
2006 Jan.29	–	2007 Feb.17	Fire
2018 Feb.16	–	2019 Feb.04	Earth
2030 Feb.02	–	2031 Jan.22	Metal

Force:	Yin
Natural element:	Metal
Season and principal month:	Autumn—October
Direction of its sign:	Northwest 60–West 20 degrees
Hours ruled by:	7P.M.–9P.M.
Best companions:	Tiger, Horse
Worst companions:	Ox, Dragon, Sheep, Rooster
Color:	Black, Dark Blue

PERSONALITY CHARACTERISTICS

Positive	Negative
Brave	Accusing
Devoted	Anxious
Discreet	Bad-tempered
Enthusiastic	Cold
Faithful	Disagreeable
Friendly	Discouraging
Helpful	Distrustful
Honest	Judgmental
Idealistic	Mean-spirited
Imaginative	Nervous
Intelligent	Pessimistic
Knowledgeable	Quarrelsome
Loyal	Strict
Modest	Suspicious
Responsible	Timid
Sensitive	
Trustworthy	
Understanding	
Unselfish	
Warmhearted	

DOG—THE ANIMAL

The close relationship between man and Dog can be traced back to ancestral times, when men went into the woods to hunt for food with a stick and the faithful Dog by their sides. Since then, Dogs have been regarded as man's best friends, and are in actuality extremely loyal and devoted.

In China, Dogs are usually associated with justice and compassion. For centuries, only the nobles could keep Dogs as pets. In fact, most Dogs were usually raised as guards and were trusted to protect their masters' welfare and property. Among the twelve animal signs, the Dog is probably the second most intelligent animal next to the brainy Monkey. Understanding, smart, and faithful, where can you find a better friend than a Dog?

Moreover, this is probably one of the most likable signs of all twelve animals. However, Dogs are often misunderstood and underrated. This can be seen in many Dog-related Chinese idioms that are mostly either negative or abusive and used to humiliate others. Luckily, Dog people are nothing like what the Chinese idioms purport.

Generally, nighttime is when a Dog is required to be alert and watchful, to guard the house and scare away any intruders. Therefore, it is believed that Dogs born in daytime will have an easier and more relaxed life than ones born at night.

DOG PEOPLE

Born under the sign of compassion and loyalty, you are honest, faithful, and sincere. In fact, in the Chinese zodiac, Dog people are probably the most humanitarian and likable of all.

You are candid and fair and exude confidence wherever you go. You respect tradition, value honor, and enjoy helping people. Not particularly sociable, you are not fond of large, noisy parties and tend to become invisible in a large crowd such as at a wedding or a big party. However, at small events your conversational skills and friendliness shine. In fact, if you could choose a way to spend the weekend, you would much rather spend a quiet afternoon tea with a close friend than go out partying till dawn.

Dog people are very righteous and are always the first to speak out against injustice. You will do everything in your power to help right the wrong. If a friend is in trouble, you will scold, complain, or even get angry, but the last thing you will do is turn away, because you simply cannot ignore a call for help. Protective and sensitive, you will protect the interests of your loved ones before your own, and are ready to jump to the defense of any family members or friends being attacked either physically or verbally.

You are truly man's best friend, and once you take someone in, this person is in for a lifetime of loyalty and devotion. Faithful and honest, you have the most profound sense of duty. You can be relied upon never to let people down. And as a good listener and an expert adviser, your many close friends highly value your opinion. Furthermore, you feel obliged to be discreet and are very reliable in keeping secrets for others. Moral and honest, you are simply not the gossiping type.

You do not like to chitchat or beat around the bush. Frank and honest, you prefer to get to the heart of the matter right away. And your quick tongue can sometimes be hurtful or sarcastic. You see things in black and white, and nothing in between.

Generally speaking, you are an agreeable companion if you are in a good mood. On the negative side, you are born anxious and worrisome, and when panic strikes, you can turn nasty and bark till everyone around you goes nuts and until you are totally out of breath. Normally, you don't hide your emotions. Happy or anxious, you show your true feelings without trying to disguise them. This makes it easy for everyone around to tell if the alarm is about to go off. Nevertheless, temperamental as you are, you are always cool in time of crises. Often you can be judgmental, defensive, and picky if someone rubs you the wrong way. Nevertheless, the Dog is not as fearsome as the Tiger, and as long as someone knows how to pet and massage you, you make absolutely the best and most honorable companion on earth.

Generally speaking, in work you need a goal to motivate you, but in reality, it is not easy for you to set a lifetime goal. However, you aren't materialistic, so money and power do not excite you. In fact, you believe it is more important to ensure the welfare of your loved ones than to pursue power and money. You usually do well in a job, and because you are very compassionate, you tend to be the type of person who will volunteer to work at a charity.

Dogs are born old and get younger as they age. Sometimes you take everything too seriously. Honesty is an important value to you, so you can't tolerate betrayal. If hurt and betrayed by any friend, you will hold the grudge all through your life and will not listen to any reasoning or explanation. A person with high morality and critical eyes, you can be pretty hard on those around you. You are honorable and trustworthy, and expect those same traits from your friends. Many times, while everyone is chatting about the weather or movie star gossip, you most likely speak up about streetlamps, complain about traffic, or social welfare. Fortunately, as you get older, it is less likely you will be so self-righteous.

Intuitive and talented, you make a splendid captain of industry, a priest, an educator, a critic, or a doctor. But whatever your career, it'll have in you a spokesman whose ideals will be profound and often original.

Dutiful and caring, you are extremely devoted when it comes to love. You tend to enter relationships in which, normally, you are the giver and the partner is the taker. You are usually very generous and loyal, and in love, you are honest and straightforward. But you will have romantic problems all your life. Really, it is mainly your own fault: You are often led by your emotional instability and your eternal anxiety. Most of the time, you can be easily agitated and extremely cynical to your partner. On the whole, you are a worrier. However, after several setbacks in relationships, when you find true love you will be a loyal husband or wife and a great parent. Nevertheless you often demand the same high degree of loyalty and devotion from your partner.

Overall, anxiety, loyalty, and protectiveness characterize the magnanimous Dog personality. Low on ego, underneath, you are a pessimist, and in time, you should learn to be less worrisome and more cautious with your hurtful tongue and words.

THE MALE DOG

Enthusiastic and noble, the male Dog is brave and candid. He is well-groomed and good-looking, extremely respectful to others, and in return he expects the same from others. Agile and attentive, he never misses any details and is famous for his keen observation. The male Dog believes in morality and takes pride in his trustworthy and candid quality. He is always the one who points out the nonsmoking sign to a smoker in the room, or speaks up when he sees someone's attempt to cut in a long line. Although he is chatty, he can still be trusted and counted on.

Always surrounded by friends, he is also popular. However, although he is reliable to his friends, he is actually quite suspicious of others. Slow to make close friends, few people are judged worthy of entering into his circle. And once you are in, you are in for life. He will be frank with you when you are wrong, and he will be ready to fight for you when you are being wronged. He is extremely protective of his loved ones, and when anything happens to these people, he takes it personally and will do anything in his power to make sure justice is served.

However, when his negative side appears, his popularity rating goes down. Always quick to criticize others and with a tendency to be cynical, he does not take criticism gracefully. When the finger is pointed at him, he can become overly defensive. This male Dog can be obstinate, judgmental and sometimes downright nasty. Moreover, he's not inclined ever to forgive and forget. When crossed, chances are he will remember it for the rest of his life and will be sarcastic whenever his enemy's name is mentioned.

Although the male Dog is sociable and enjoys spending time with his friends, he prefers a one-on-one dinner to going out to a big party. Not particularly adventurous, Dog man is happier going to a movie or a good restaurant than rafting or rock climbing. In fact, he can be considered adventurous when it comes to food. He enjoys foreign cuisine and is not afraid to try exotic food such as Ethiopian or Mongolian.

Usually animated and attractive, Dog man has a unique sense of humor. Some might consider him weird, but no one complains, and, most people enjoy his peculiarity. He is very committed to his lover during courtship and marriage. An ideal life partner, this loyal man nevertheless can be temperamental at times.

THE FEMALE DOG

Gifted and creative, the female Dog is smart, intelligent, and fun. She is usually quite attractive and enjoys stimulating conversation. She is not materialistic and doesn't care much for power and money.

Friendly and honest, she is a direct person who does not skirt around the issues. She always speaks her mind without hesitation and stands up for her principles when she sees injustice. Courageous and righteous, she has a strong sense of morality and feels it is her duty to right the wrongs and fight for principles. Although she speaks frankly about what she believes, she is also wise enough to listen to other people before making a final decision or drawing a conclusion on her own. She is straightforward and has no interest in psychological game playing or manipulation. For her, what you see is what you get, so she'll never be as secretive as the female Snake; nevertheless, she is discreet enough for you to trust her with your deepest secret.

As an individualist, she doesn't blindly follow fashion. Witty and idealistic, she knows what she wants in life and is usually more ambitious than the male Dog.

Sharon Stone, Cher, and Jamie Lee Curtis are just three famous Dog women.

The female Dog sometimes gives the impression of being cold or indifferent to disguise her anxiety and worrisome nature. A pessimist at heart, she thinks the worst is yet to come and is constantly anxious and doubtful about her own ability.

She is very capable and genuinely feels she knows what's best. Although she might appear calm and restful at times, this female Dog rarely relaxes. In fact, before she meets her friends at the movies, she has probably already been to the drugstore to pick up some aspirin and the cleaners to drop off her dirty laundry. And while she is watching the movie, her mind has already wandered outside the theater, wondering if she remembered to mail a package, if the phone bill is due, and if it is about time to give her dog a bath. This female Dog is a multitasker, and her heart and mind are always jumping.

Like most Dogs, the idealist female Dog can be cynical and critical. She believes everyone should live by her high standards. She has to be right and doesn't allow criticism and compromise. And when challenged about her principles, she can be downright judgmental and obstinate.

In relationships, she is devoted and loyal. As a person who speaks her mind, she is always the first one to confess her love or to break up. An ideal wife to most men, she is faithful and caring; an ideal mother to her children, she is playful and affectionate and knows how to communicate with her kids. In general, the female Dog needs to learn to be less picky and understand that not everyone should follow her rules.

DOG AT WORK

Capable and knowledgeable, Dog people are in high demand in the job market. Their loyalty and sense of responsibility are legendary, and their devotion is without question. They exude confidence wherever they go and are admired for their bravery and dignity.

Dogs like to work, and whatever career they choose, they want to be the expert in the field. Friendly and helpful, the Dog can easily make friends. A good judge of character, Dog people are very observant and alert. Sometimes, they might be a bit too suspicious of others. Nevertheless, they can count on their intuition to help in making decisions. And because of their ability and loyalty, they are usually trusted and given important responsibilities.

As a boss, Dogs feel right at home because being picky and somewhat bossy is second nature to them. They will be devoted bosses and will speak up without hesitation when they see faults. However, they are still accessible to their staffs and can be helpful and understanding.

As a partner, Dogs are extremely loyal. They are definitely not the kind of partners who will turn their back on the other partner and trade behind his back. Although they think they know the best, fortunately, they are also open-minded and welcome any friendly advice. In times of crisis, they appear calm although inside they are panicking. Avoid pointing fingers at them because any criticism or accusation will bring out the worst in him or her and perhaps lead to the end of this partnership.

As a colleague, Dog people are famous for their loyalty. They are the kind of coworkers who will give a helping hand or a shoulder to cry on whenever needed. Most of the time, they put the interests of others ahead of their own. Even if coworkers feel flattered or guilty, they shouldn't try to stop Dogs, because personal relationships mean a great deal to them. Helping their coworkers gives Dogs a great sense of achievement and happiness.

Generally speaking, with their sensitive and compassionate heart, Dogs will do well as charity workers, doctors, missionaries, or teachers. Mother Teresa, Prince William, and Winston Churchill are just three famous Dog people.

BEST DOG OCCUPATIONS

Actor	Nurse
Charity worker	Philosopher
Critic	Police officer
Doctor	Politician
Educator	Priest
FBI agent	Researcher
Judge	Scientist
Lawyer	Social worker
Legal aid lawyer	Teacher
Missionary	Trade union leader
Nun	Writer

FAMOUS DOGS

Andre Agassi	Mariah Carey
Bill Clinton	Michael Jackson
Cher	Mother Teresa
Elvis Presley	Prince William
George Gershwin	Sharon Stone
Jamie Lee Curtis	Winston Churchill

COMPATIBILITY

The Chinese believe each animal sign is most compatible with signs that are four years apart, and least compatible with the sign that is six years apart. Based on this concept, a circle can be drawn with all signs, locating the Triangle of Affinity and the Circle of Conflict.

TRIANGLE OF AFFINITY
Dog, Tiger, Horse are the Triangle of Affinity

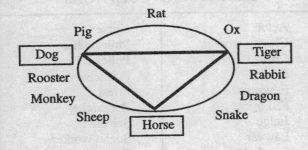

CIRCLE OF CONFLICT
Dog's sign of conflict is Dragon

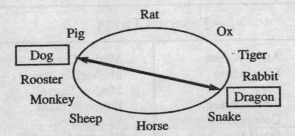

Signs	Rating 1–10	Relationship
Dog with Rat	7	Why not
Dog with Ox	5	This is one rocky relationship
Dog with Tiger	8	Good—a balanced and harmonious relationship
Dog with Rabbit	7	As long as they don't take each other for granted
Dog with Dragon	*4*	*Believe me you can do better than that*
Dog with Snake	7	A balanced and compatible team
Dog with Horse	9	A happy couple
Dog with Sheep	6	Difficult relationship
Dog with Monkey	6	With reservations—the Dog might suffer
Dog with Rooster	6	Only if it's absolutely necessary
Dog with Dog	7	They understand each other but love to fight
Dog with Pig	7	They share their thoughts and feelings

Dog with Rat   7
Why not

The Rat and the Dog respect each other and can be an amicable couple. The Dog and the Rat are both responsible and diligent, and they both take the relationship seriously. Sometimes, Rats might find it difficult to understand the sentimental Dog, for they can be too generous and tend to give money away. However, the practical Rat will be anxious over the money and try to save as much as possible. In the end, these two will know how to resolve their problems and learn from each other.

Dog with Ox   5
This is one rocky relationship

These two don't have much in common, and the Dog might suffer in this Ox-Dog union. Both loyal and hard-working, these two seem similar at the first glance, but the truth is, they can battle over the silliest topic. The witty Dog will criticize the serious Ox for lacking a sense of humor, and the practical Ox will complain about the charitable Dog and his or her unrealistic desire to save the world. The Ox will be counting the dimes for rainy days, while the Dog will try to persuade the Ox to donate some to Greenpeace. This is a couple with a rocky start and a lot to overcome.

Dog with Tiger   8
Good—a balanced and harmonious relationship

Both are perfectionists. The Tiger and the Dog actually seem to know a way to get along perfectly. The understanding Dog knows how to handle the impulsive and playful Tiger, and the Tiger appreciates the Dog's loyalty and sensibility. Both are frank and sincere; they will not hide away from confrontation when something becomes a problem for them. Best of all, these two types will not hold grudges against each other or let one dominate the other. This will be a balanced and long-lasting rela-

tionship, and each will benefit from the partner's talents
and experience.

Dog with Rabbit   7
As long as they don't take each other for granted

The combination of the Rabbit and the Dog will work out
just fine. Both the Rabbit and the Dog will feel comfortable enough to share their thoughts and feelings with
each other, and will have a basic understanding of their
strengths and weaknesses. The Dog depends on the practical Rabbit to set their goals and priorities, and the
Rabbit admires the Dog's loyalty and sincerity. These two
types get along well together, and despite their small differences, as long as they don't take each other for granted
they can be a great team.

Dog with Dragon   4
Believe me you can do better than that

This is definitely not a recommended relationship. The
naïve Dragon has tons of grand plans that the Dog will
not hesitate to criticize and deflate the Dragon's big ego.
At the same time, the Dragon cannot stand the cynical
Dog and dislikes to be questioned on every one of his or
her dreams. Also, there is a serious communication
problem between these two. Each partner will misinterpret most of the things said, and it's not a pretty picture
to see a fuming Dragon arguing with a barking Dog. It
might be smarter to stay away from each other.

Dog with Snake   7
A balanced and compatible team

The Snake and the Dog will get along fine together. The Dog admires the Snake's intelligence and talents while the Snake is touched by the Dog's loyalty and dedication. This will be a balanced and compatible team. Both are idealistic and have a mutual understanding of each other's weaknesses and strengths. The Dog is smart to overlook the Snake's secretive and selfish nature, and in return, the Snake learns to accept the Dog's nagging. If they have similar goals to work toward, they are most likely to succeed.

Dog with Horse   9
A happy couple

This is a great example of the opposite attraction. The Horse and the Dog don't appear to share anything in common, but, in fact, their differences will complement each other just fine. The Horse is independent and aggressive, and the Dog is generous and sensitive. The loyal Dog will not mind the Horse's dominance and will follow the Horse on their travels. The Horse appreciates the Dog's communicative and considerate nature and finds it easy to share thoughts and ideas with the Dog. Neither of them is competitive, and they will enjoy each other's company while maintaining their own independence. They make a happy couple.

Dog with Sheep   6
Difficult relationship

The combination of the Sheep and the Dog spells difficulty. The Sheep is very dependent and demands all of the

Dog's attention and dedication. Fortunately, the Dog is very tolerant and sympathetic, and will try his or her very best to fulfill the Sheep's wishes. However, the Sheep will keep testing the limits of the Dog's tolerance, eventually bringing out the negative traits of the Dog. In the end, both the Sheep and the Dog will find each other irritating.

Dog with Monkey   6
With reservations—the Dog might suffer

These two seem like a perfect match for each other; one possesses qualities lacking in the other. But truthfully, the Dog is easygoing and kind, and the sociable and lively Monkey can be both charming and manipulative. Take a guess at who is dominant in the relationship. . . . The pessimistic Dog will let the Monkey take control and lead the way, but will expect the flirtatious and fickle Monkey to be loyal and honest in the relationship. Actually, this union can become great friends, although love is possible between these two, the Dog might be disappointed and suffer.

Dog with Rooster   6
Only if it's absolutely necessary

The Rooster and the Dog don't always see eye to eye. The Dog usually finds the Rooster argumentative and unkind, while the Rooster simply cannot stand the Dog's high moral standards. This will not be a balanced relationship since the Rooster will be very aggressive and expects the tolerant Dog to support his or her every single decision and move. The Dog will try to understand and be supportive, but eventually his or her patience will run out, and they will end up being apart.

Dog with Dog　　　6
They understand each other but love to fight

When two Dogs join together, they will find each other warm and understanding. Both are accountable and honest, they share the same moral standards, and are committed to their action and duty. They like to work as a team and will respect each other's decisions and judgments. Nonetheless, there will still be some struggles for dominance. And if one rubs the other the wrong way, their argumentative nature will take over, and a barking contest will begin.

Dog with Pig　　　7
They share their thoughts and feelings

The Dog will have a wonderful relationship with the Pig. Both honest and sincere, the Pig and the Dog find it easy to communicate and share their thoughts and feelings with each other. The optimistic Pig can teach the sometimes overly serious Dog how to loosen up a little bit, and the Dog will be protective of the Pig. There will be no major conflict between the two, and this union will benefit the Dog the most. It will be a lasting relationship.

THE FIVE ELEMENTS:
The Dog—the natural element is Metal

THE METAL DOG: 1910, 1970, 2030

The Metal Dog is in its natural element and the Chinese consider this double-Metal sign to be the "Iron Dog." In ancient China, the Metal Dog could be either very good or very bad, depending on whether it takes the positive or negative course. The double-Metal strengthens the Dog's idealistic quality. The Metal Dogs usually have very high standards, are extremely opinionated, and sometimes take things too seriously. Nevertheless, the Metal Dog can be selflessly dedicated to objects or people worthy of devotion, and at the same time, ruthlessly pursue enemies when provoked. Decisive, loyal Dogs will pick a side immediately and never desert their affiliations.

THE WATER DOG: 1922, 1982, 2042

The Water element softens the Dog's rough edges and creates a sympathetic and pleasant Dog. Water Dogs are usually popular; they are very diplomatic and easygoing. Though usually more liberal and flexible than other Dogs, this makes it hard for them to be good leaders or managers sometimes. They like to indulge themselves and others to self-gratification, and can be very sympathetic to those who are on the opposite side. Some believe that Water Dog is the most charming and sensual of all animal signs. They are fluent in expressing themselves and can be great counselors.

THE WOOD DOG: 1874, 1934, 1994

The Wood element brings warmth and stability to the Dog's nature. Wood Dogs are generous, kind, and energetic, which makes them comfortable coworkers in a team environment. They usually form long-lasting and loyal relationships with those they choose to befriend or love. Wood Dogs are drawn to money, success, and art. They are not necessarily very creative themselves, but they know how to appreciate. Sometimes too eager to please, the Wood Dog can be indecisive if he or she lacks support or approval from others.

THE FIRE DOG: 1886, 1946, 2006

The Fire element revitalizes the Fire Dog and creates an attractive and popular individual. Fire Dogs are more approachable than other Dogs and are very friendly and charismatic. Often in the center of the limelight, they can easily convince others to follow their lead and are very popular with the opposite sex. Fire Dogs often need mentors to learn from and guide them. This is probably why they often relate better to people older than themselves. Fire Dogs love new experiences and seek adventures; they are curious and enthusiastic and often succeed at any project they have in mind.

THE EARTH DOG: 1898, 1958, 2018

Earth Dogs are well-balanced people. They are faithful to their own beliefs, but will also agree with the majority; they are idealistic like most Dogs, but the Earth element makes them practical enough so they don't lose sight of reality. Earth Dogs have high moral standards and the tendency to demand the same dedication and loyalty from others. Unlike other Dogs, the Earth Dogs are less anxious about the future, and instead take one day at a time to fight and to survive. They are the thinkers in the Dog family.

The Chivalrous Pig

Ranking order   Twelfth

YEARS   ## ELEMENTS

1911 Jan.30	–	1912 Feb.17	Metal
1923 Feb.16	–	1924 Feb.04	Water
1935 Feb.04	–	1936 Jan.23	Wood
1947 Jan.22	–	1948 Feb.09	Fire
1959 Feb.08	–	1960 Jan.27	Earth
1971 Jan.27	–	1972 Feb.14	Metal
1983 Feb.13	–	1984 Feb.01	Water
1995 Jan.31	–	1996 Feb.18	Wood
2007 Feb.18	–	2008 Feb.08	Fire

Force:	**Yin**
Natural element:	**Water**
Season and principal month:	**Autumn——November**
Direction of its sign:	**North 30° by Northwest**
Hours ruled by:	**9P.M.–11P.M.**
Best companions:	**Sheep, Rabbit**
Worst companions:	**Snake, Monkey, Pig**
Color:	**Black**

PERSONALITY CHARACTERISTICS

Positive	Negative
Affectionate	Competitive
Amusing	Fearful
Caring	Hesitant
Charitable	Hot-tempered
Cheerful	Impatient
Courteous	Indulgent
Determined	Materialistic
Forgiving	Naïve
Generous	Pessimistic
Honest	Sardonic
Knowledgeable	Snide
Obliging	Snobbish
Optimistic	Spendthrift
Outgoing	Stingy
Peaceful	
Self-sacrificing	
Sensible	
Smart	
Talented	

PIG—THE ANIMAL

The most famous pig in Chinese literature is probably the
Pig Man character in the *Monkey King* story; one of the
most renowned classical novels in Chinese history, also
known as *Journey to the West*.

This imaginative fiction was actually based on a true story of a famous Chinese monk, Xuan Zang (602–664) who traveled on foot all the way to India and finally brought back the Buddhist holy book.

In the story, the Pig Man character escorts and protects the monk during his journey. Originally a heavenly general, the Pig Man was sent down to the world as punishment for his crime of assaulting a fairy. As a comic sidekick in the story, the Pig Man is not as powerful and mischievous as the Monkey King. Instead, he is gullible and indulgent. Though he appears to be courageous, he has two major weaknesses—food and women. His enemies often set these up as bait and succeed in trapping him with minimal effort. Nevertheless, despite all the obstacles he experienced during the trip, the loyal Pig Man still guarded and protected the monk all through the journey and eventually completed his mission and returned with the holy book. *Journey to the West* is probably one of the most imaginative works in Chinese literature and is definitely worth reading.

PIG PEOPLE

Pig people are one of the rare gems among the twelve animal signs. Unlike Western culture, which associates Pigs with laziness and sloppiness, Chinese astrology sees Pigs as some of the most sincere and genuine people. You are the type of person everyone admires most, and many friends consider you some of the nicest, most loving and caring people around.

You are generous, affectionate, and sensual to a fault; it is no wonder you are quite popular among friends.

People born in the year of Pig have a heart of gold. You are the ones leaned on when people need a shoulder to cry on, the counselor called upon when sincere advice is needed, and the one who'll always give a helping hand to those who need you. No wonder the Chinese zodiac defines Pig people as the best friends anyone can have.

You are quite famous for your hospitality. "To love, to give, and to share" is probably the motto you've lived by. Since childhood, you've had an innocent outlook on life— you truly believe the best of mankind and refuse to see otherwise. No one, not even serial killers, can sway you from your belief in the basic good-hearted nature of all men and women. Truthfully, no matter how old you are, you will probably stay just as naïve and good-hearted.

Sometimes, people can't help but wonder if you really exist because you seem too good to be true. Born under the sign of honesty, you are incapable of telling a lie. Even if you think about lying, your conscience will force you to tell the truth. And when you absolutely must tell a "white lie," the guilt you feel inside will tear you apart for days. So you think and trust like a saint, but you certainly don't live like one. Social events and parties are the favorite activities for the fun-loving Pig like you. Truly, no party will be complete without the warm, amusing Pig. Better yet, you definitely know how to throw a good party as its spectacular host or hostess.

You are quite self-indulgent when it comes to your own needs. You don't worry about spending money. Actually, your lifestyle can be quite extravagant, enjoying expensive furniture and fancy sports cars. You know how to have a good time and constantly seek pleasure. Pleasuring your senses—for instance, eating Häagen-Dazs ice cream, lobster, and after-dinner chocolates—is important to you. As someone who was born in the year of the Pig, your hefty appetite should not surprise you. But Pig people do not stuff themselves with greasy food like hamburgers and fries. You prefer dining in the best restaurants in town. And even if you do overeat, at least you eat with good taste. You're quite picky about the quality of the food, which fits with your strong sense of luxury.

However, most of the time, as a Pig person you feel that it is your responsibility to keep everyone happy, which is probably why you are quite bad in the art of saying "No" to others. Admit it, you were probably crowned "Mr. Nice Guy" or "Miss Nice Girl" in high school. You often sacrifice your own happiness, interests, and comfort for the sake of someone else. Your friends often put their trust in you because they know you won't let them down. Pig people are easygoing and honest, and simply want everything to be done right.

You are a caring friend, so if you invite someone into your circle, he or she will be in for a lifetime of a loyal, faithful, and giving friendship. For those lucky friends of the Pig people, remember never to try to force your opinion on a Pig friend. A Pig rarely asks for help and can't graciously accept it. You can be really stubborn. Once you've made up your mind on something, it is unlikely anyone or anything can change your mind.

Everyone knows you are naïve but your innocence can sometimes exceed imagination. Unfortunately, because of your trusting nature, many people take advantage of you. You may often find yourself being deceived, disappointed, swindled, and hurt. But your biggest problem is that you forgive too easily. If friends hurt your feelings, you will find all kinds of excuses for their behavior right away, and if this happens too often, then you will think it

is your fault instead of theirs. You are often more forgiving of others than of yourself. Sensual and affectionate
as you seem, it is not wise to rub you the wrong way. If a
Pig is being forced into a corner, he or she can be extremely vengeful and will not hesitate to fight back.
Luckily, the Pig has a big heart and doesn't usually hold
a grudge for long.

Like the Monkey, you are intelligent, erudite, and have
a great thirst for knowledge. You are the people who sub-
scribe to dozens of magazines, from *National Geographic*
to *Newton*, just so you can always be up-to-date. You
don't usually say much—but when you do decide to
speak, suddenly, nothing can stop you until you run out of
subjects.

You are hardworking, optimistic and determined,
which is probably why you usually succeed in your
career. In relationships, you are sensitive, sweet, caring
though naïve. You are a romantic in heart and certainly
the marrying kind. But on the negative side, you can also
be possessive, and jealous.

THE MALE PIG

In the Disney animated movie, *The Lion King*, Pumbaa,
the wild boar, is one carefree little fellow. Simple, honest,
and cheerful, he is also friendly, gullible, and has the appetite of an elephant and the courage of a tiger. Sound familiar? Look no further—he is just like the long-lost twin
brother of the male Pig. They share so many similarities
in personality traits.

Fortunately, none of the male Pigs is a chauvinist pig.
In fact, he is very sensitive and caring. Like a true gen-

tleman, he has an impeccable manner and a generous soul. Outgoing and fun, he is a partygoer and is quite popular. Nevertheless, some think him a little bit snobbish when the truth is, he is simply an aesthete. He enjoys the fine things in life, such as good food and fine wines, and he is born with an excellent eye for style.

Like most Pigs, he is kindhearted, friendly, affectionate, and sensible. He is endowed with common sense, but he is not good at reading people. He can be easily deceived and yet he seems to forgive and forget as easily and always manages to stand up again after being struck down by others. Nevertheless, his endurance and forgiveness will not tolerate those who try to ruin his reputation. Once provoked, the male Pig can be extremely vicious and aggressive. He will throw away his happy, jolly-fellow outlook, stand up, and retaliate vigorously, until his rival eventually waves the white flag and gives up.

The male Pig could be a great follower of Mencius, the pupil of Confucius, who has preached all his life in the belief that all men and women are born kind. Loyal and cheerful, he only sees the best in mankind. However, he resents being called naïve. Over and over again, the male Pig is duped and then complains about it, and then the cycle starts all over again. Although he doesn't seem to learn from his errors, he actually does wise up little by little. The male Pig seems hesitant at times, and grows suspicious after being betrayed and victimized once too often.

The male Pig loves to please people, and he makes it seem so effortless and natural to do so. He cares a great deal about his image and how others view him, which makes him more vulnerable and gullible. It is easy to make a Pig feel guilty because he is so eager to please everyone, especially the ones he loves.

The male Pig is quite attractive and is certainly not short of female admirers; yet he seems vulnerable even in his love relationships. Affectionate and loving, he can fall in and out of love quickly, but being hurt and betrayed repeatedly will not stop him in his search for a soul mate. He loves being in love and will not be discouraged by some frustrating experiences. Although the popular male Pig seems to date a lot before settling down, he is a loyal husband. Once a male Pig is committed to a relationship, he will be faithful and devoted to his family.

THE FEMALE PIG

The female Pig always shows up with a smile. She is cheerful, considerate, and honest. People are drawn to her by her friendliness and, once invited into the female Pig's circle of friends, are in for a lifetime of her devotion and sacrifice. The female Pig always goes the extra mile to help her friends, even if that means sacrificing her own happiness and comfort.

Although she loves to help people, when it comes to her own problems she can be extremely stubborn and refuse to take any help. It takes time for a female Pig to learn to open up and talk about her problems. But who can blame her? After being deceived and betrayed once too many times, the gullible female Pig builds up a defense mechanism and learns not to confide too easily.

So it makes sense that she can be extremely shy and inhibited when it comes to love. The Pig woman tends to hide her true feelings deep inside unless she feels certain that the object of her affection shares the same feelings for her. She is never the aggressor in the relationship; after all, our Miss Piggy is a romantic at heart and prefers to be pampered, courted, and swooned.

She is innocent, sympathetic, and generous, thus making her the perfect target for those who are unscrupulous. Good friends of the Pig woman will understand this. She'll probably often talk about her frustrating relationship, and no matter how many times she is warned, she'll stay with him and will cry to her friends again when she is left alone again. It can be somewhat painful to be a friend of a Pig woman, seeing the heartbreak coming, but being unable to do anything to stop it.

Despite her problems with relationships, the Pig woman is generally clever and bright. She loves social events and knows how to enjoy herself at a party. Shopping is second nature to her; she buys expensive gifts for her friends, purchases Gucci or LV handbags for her sisters, and orders luxury drapes for her living room. She is the kind of person who picks up the item she likes and puts it into the shopping basket without even bothering to check the price.

Miss Piggy will have a good life; her good luck always helps her when she needs it. Money will be comfortable, as long as she tames her urges to go on shopping sprees. And in love, she must learn to listen to her friends once in a while and protect herself from those who exploit her.

PIG AT WORK

For centuries Pig people have been given a bad rap. But finally, the time has come to help the world understand

Pig people. "No, they are not sloppy, and no, they are not lazy."

In fact, Pig people are great assets to any company, which explains why Pigs are rarely unemployed. They are very hardworking and diligent, have a thirst for knowledge, and are often very erudite and talented. And, whenever they think it is time to make a career move, their natural good luck waves a new and better job opportunity in front of them.

To Pig people, there is a big equals sign between their emotional security and their financial security. Although they don't care that much about power and money, they do want to live a lavish lifestyle. After all, window-shopping is never the same as a real shopping bag full of wonderful stuff in one's hands. And this need for a certain lifestyle pushes them to work harder than others.

As a boss or manager, the Pig is energetic and involved, and surprisingly, very approachable. They are caring and generous to their colleagues, and determined and diligent as anyone on their staff. Really, no one has as much talent in people skills as Pig people. They don't intimidate their staff like the Dragons, nor do they manipulate the staff like the Monkeys. In fact, they treat their staff with genuine friendliness and sincerity. However, on the negative side, the Pig boss can be temperamental and impulsive at times, and when they change their minds, they won't be swayed easily. Fortunately, the Pig boss is also fair, so as long as their subordinates don't force their ideas on their Pig bosses or start a big argument with them, the Pig boss will listen and give in eventually.

As a colleague, the Pig is everyone's best friend and a supportive team member. He is completely devoted and will sacrifice his own welfare for others. He is the kind of person who works over the weekend to finish other people's work and still comes in early Monday morning with bagels to share. Who wouldn't love him?

In general, Pigs' love for food and luxury makes them excellent chefs or restaurant owners. And with their charisma and popularity, they can also make great politicians or administrative officers. Henry Kissinger, Ronald Reagan, and the Dalai Lama are just three famous Pig people.

BEST PIG OCCUPATIONS

Administrative officer	Painter
Builder	Personnel manager
Chef	Researcher
Chemist	Restaurateur
Civil servant	Scientist
Delicatessen owner	Shoemaker
Doctor	Social worker
Engineer	Technician
Fundraiser	Writer
Musician	

FAMOUS PIGS

Alfred Hitchcock	Luciano Pavarotti
Chiang Kai-shek	Richard Dreyfuss
Billy Crystal	Ronald Reagan
Elton John	Sonny Bono
Ernest Hemingway	Stephen King
Henry Kissinger	Steven Spielberg
Hillary Rodham Clinton	the Dalai Lama
Julie Andrews	Woody Allen
John D. Rockefeller	Winona Ryder
Kevin Kline	

COMPATIBILITY

The Chinese believe each animal sign is most compatible with signs that are four years apart, and least compatible with the sign that is six years apart. Based on this concept, a circle can be drawn with all signs, locating the Triangle of Affinity and the Circle of Conflict.

TRIANGLE OF AFFINITY
Pig, Rabbit, Sheep are the Triangle of Affinity

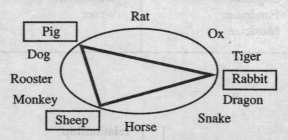

CIRCLE OF CONFLICT
Pig's conflict sign is Snake

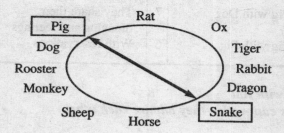

Signs	Rating 1–10	Relationship
Pig with Rat	8	This can work—they admire each other
Pig with Ox	6	Why not it's worth a try
Pig with Tiger	7	They are very different, but this will work
Pig with Rabbit	9	Very compatible—they will be happy together
Pig with Dragon	7	Balanced but not passionate
Pig with Snake	4	*The Pig can never please the Snake*
Pig with Horse	7	This relationship is worth a try
Pig with Sheep	9	One of the happiest possible combinations
Pig with Monkey	6	Not a balanced relationship

Pig with Rooster	7	The Pig is patient—it could work
Pig with Dog	7	They share their thoughts and feelings
Pig with Pig	6	With reservations

Pig with Rat   *8*
This can work—they admire each other

It is nice to see a positive relationship like this. The Rat and the Pig are both sociable and affectionate, and they will adore and respect each other. They make a good team and are usually well connected and influential. The couple share the same passion for good food and vacation, and try to enjoy life as much as they can. The Pig is generous and sometimes has a great appetite for shopping. The Rat, however, is practical and thrifty. In order to balance the relationship and their bank account, the Rat must take control over the purse and let the Pig charm the rest of the world.

Pig with Ox   *6*
Why not, it's worth a try

The Ox-Pig combination can be an interesting one. The disciplined Ox will most likely be the one that takes control in the couple. After all, the easygoing Pig will probably rather be hanging out with friends than spending time at a desk filing a tax return. It is no surprise to learn that the Ox enjoys staying in on a beautiful Sunday morning, reading a nice book or simply just sleeping in.

On the contrary, the Pig will start calling up every single friend to arrange a picnic by the lake or all-night dancing at a nightclub. Despite the differences, this partnership definitely deserves a chance to succeed.

Pig with Tiger   7
They are very different, but this will work

When you see both the Tiger and the Pig in the same room, you know what it means—party time! These two are both popular, social animals. Worry-free and fun-loving, the Tiger and the Pig are both affectionate and gregarious. The combination of the Tiger and the Pig can be a good one because they can cooperate with and support each other. They may appear different at first glance; however, they will learn to appreciate each other and eventually develop a better way to communicate.

Pig with Rabbit   9
Very compatible—they will be happy together

This is probably one of the best combinations for the Pig. Rabbits and Pigs are extremely compatible, and they both take time to understand each other. The Rabbit is intelligent and keen to understand the strengths and weaknesses of the Pig, and the Pig will rely on the practical Rabbit for advice and decisions. This couple knows how to appreciate the contribution of each other and how to tolerate each other's likes and dislikes. Most of the time, the sociable Pig will be the spokesperson, while the Rabbit will be the organizer. The combination of the Rabbit and the Pig will be long-lasting and fun-loving.

Pig with Dragon   7
Balanced but not passionate

Although the Dragon and the Pig do not share much in
common, these two will have a balanced relationship.
They are probably not as passionate as some of the other
combinations are, but at least they will respect and admire
each other. The Pig adores the confident Dragon and welcomes the leadership from the Dragon; in the meantime,
the Dragon appreciates the honest and easygoing nature
of the Pig. Of course, the Dragon can be a little egotistical
when compared with the Pig's big, charitable heart. Nevertheless, they will be compatible and enjoy each other's
companionship building a long-lasting relationship.

Pig with Snake   4
The Pig can never please the Snake

For a Snake and a Pig, opposite attraction will never
work. Being the conflicted opposites, the Snake and the
Pig tend to see only the faults in each other. The Pig will
be annoyed by the Snake's secretive and jealous personality, and the Snake will find the Pig naïve and careless.
After all, the cautious Snake always observes and plans
everything in detail, and the fact that the Pig often dives
into any relationship without suspicion can be disturbing
to the Snake. Although forgiving and enduring, the Pig
will find it a mission impossible to please the Snake.

Pig with Horse   7
This relationship is worth a try

The Horse and the Pig seem to get along just fine. The
popular and sociable Pig enjoys parties, as does the fun-

loving Horse. The Horse enjoys the Pig's generous and affectionate nature, while the Pig finds the Horse's independence attractive. However, both the Horse and the Pig are stubborn and cannot be rubbed the wrong way; the mischievous Horse may try to test the limits of the Pig's tolerance. In order to succeed, the couple needs to communicate better and learn to compromise with each other.

Pig with Sheep   9
One of the happiest possible combinations

Congratulations! The Sheep-Pig couple is probably one of the happiest combinations in Chinese astrology. Both are sociable and sensitive; the Sheep and the Pig share a lot in common and dearly appreciate each other. This couple has a mutual understanding and can benefit a great deal from each other's talents and personality. Both seek harmony and a peaceful life, they don't argue much, and will usually sort out their problems in a calm and reasonable way. Just a little reminder for the couple: Be more conservative with your spending and your lavish lifestyle.

Pig with Monkey   6
Not a balanced relationship

Both are optimistic and friendly, both are popular and sociable, so the Monkey and the Pig can be a great team. In this relationship, they will enjoy each other's company and can always learn and benefit from the other. Hopefully, the Pig will not mind the Monkey's plans and schemes, and the Monkey will be able to help and support the Pig. As long as they have the same vision and interests, these two can make great friends and lovers.

Pig with Rooster   7
The Pig is patient—it could work

The Rooster and the Pig work well together as a couple. The Pig does not mind the Rooster's controlling nature, and the Rooster finds the Pig generous and sensitive. These two can be both good friends and compatible lovers. There might be some trouble when conflict arrives, as the Rooster and the Pig approach problems from different angles. Nevertheless, the Pig is very patient and sympathetic, and will put up with the Rooster's criticism and eventually calm him or her down.

Pig with Dog   7
They share their thoughts and feelings

The Dog will have a wonderful relationship with the Pig. Both of them are honest and sincere, so they find it easy to communicate and share their thoughts and feelings with each other. The optimistic Pig can teach the sometimes too serious Dog how to loosen up, and the Dog will be protective of the Pig. There will be no major conflict between the two, and this union will benefit the Dog the most. It will be a lasting relationship.

Pig with Pig   6
With reservations

The relationship between two Pigs is not necessarily a compatible one. While sharing the same negative and positive traits, the two Pigs seem to understand each other but fail to tolerate their faults. Strangely, the Pig-Pig combination seems to bring out their worst, selfish sides. There will be misunderstandings as well as misinterpretation between the two, and both will be unwilling to resolve their problems. This is a relationship to be entered into with many reservations.

THE FIVE ELEMENTS:
The Pig—the natural element is Water

THE METAL PIG: 1911, 1971, 2031

The Metal element makes people born under the Pig sign more stubborn and ambitious. This type of Pig does not take failure or defeat gracefully. But don't worry, as an active doer with strength and intelligence, Metal Pig is never a quitter. The Metal Pigs are sociable and popular and very affectionate and trusting toward their friends. You can literally read them like an open book, which is not always a good thing. Often betrayed by friends, the Metal Pigs need to realize that not all friends will return the same honesty and sincerity for their friendship.

THE WATER PIG: 1863, 1923, 1983

Since the Pig's natural element is Water, the double-Water elements strengthen their sensibility and keen observation, which helps them see through an opponent's desires and weaknesses; they are also diplomatic and sympathetic people and excellent negotiators. Water Pigs love to party, and are passionate and affectionate with their loved ones. Their weakness is their tendency to indulge their desires and hobbies. They are the believers in "see no evil, hear no evil," and refuse to talk badly about anybody. This makes them vulnerable to others, and they can be used or betrayed if not careful. Water Pigs should try to be more in touch with reality.

THE WOOD PIG: 1875, 1935, 1995

Communicative and good-hearted, the Wood Pig is gifted at bringing people together. They are wise and give good advice. Although they can be interested in their own gains, Wood Pigs are usually sympathetic and will devote time and effort to social and charity events. They get along well with everyone and are often organizers for social functions. Wood Pigs are persuasive people who can easily encourage others to support them wholeheartedly. Yet like all Pigs, the Wood Pigs should be cautious about whom they associate with and learn to be choosier with friends instead of placing blind faith in every stranger.

THE FIRE PIG: 1887, 1947, 2007

The Fire element makes the Pig daring and courageous. Possessed with intense emotions and determination, Fire Pigs are the wanna-be heroes. Like all Pigs, they are idealistic, and are so optimistic that they look forward to the unknown future. Sometimes they can be too optimistic and are constantly testing their luck. Fire Pigs are loving and sincere people who trust people easily without putting any guard in between. People born under this sign can be powerful and willful, capable of reaching great heights of achievement or great depths of degradation.

THE EARTH PIG: 1899, 1959, 2019

The Earth element gives the Pig a sense of steadiness and patience. Earth Pigs are usually very productive and have great willpower, coping with stress and burdens that most people can't endure. They are ambitious, but are aware of their own limits. Earth Pigs are constantly seeking security and are resourceful, self-confident, and hardworking, physically fit, and full of stamina. In general, Earth Pigs are reliable associates, helpful employers, as well as kind, considerate friends.

Acknowledgments

No book is the creation of one person, and there was no way I could complete this book without the help and inspiration of others. Therefore, I'd like to express my sincere gratitude to:

Eva, Philip and Reggero: my old friends, for suggesting Chinese for dinner that night and for your suggestion, which eventually led to the creation of the "Sabrina's Chinese Astrology Web Site".

NYU Center for Advanced Technology and especially to Ken and Clilly: my good friends, for my site cannot possibly stay alive without the encouragement and support you have given me through the years.

Reena: my dear friend, for bringing the writer out of me by being a creative and inspiring author/producer herself.

Richard and Yolanda: my favorite couple, for letting me invade your sweet home and PC so I could still write while traveling in Europe.

Hon Yo Liu: my genius uncle-in-law, for giving me help and consultation and for sharing insight on your research on the Chinese zodiac and Yi-Ching.

Jackie Joiner: my brilliant editor, for scouring me out through the Internet and for your courage and patience to take on this task. I have learned a lot from you.

Visitors to my web site: Thanks for visiting and returning to my site each year and especially to those who took their time to sign my guestbook with their thoughts, praise, and suggestions.

Dad, Mommy, Eliza, and Gilly: my dearest family, for being there for me whenever I need you and for your unconditional love and support through the years. I am truly thankful for having you as my family.